Shining
Art on Light

Shining Art on Light

Colorful Insights

———

JAMES T. DAKIN

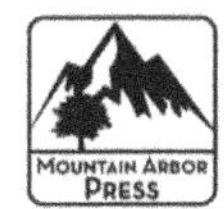

MOUNTAIN ARBOR
PRESS *an Imprint of BookLogix*

Alpharetta, Georgia

Copyright © 2024 by James T. Dakin

All rights reserved. No part of this book may be reproduced or transmitted in any form or by any means, electronic or mechanical, including photocopying, recording, or any information storage and retrieval system, without permission in writing from the author.

ISBN: 978-1-6653-0889-2 - Paperback
eISBN: 978-1-6653-0890-8 - eBook

These ISBNs are the property of Mountain Arbor Press (a Division of BookLogix) for the express purpose of sales and distribution of this title. The content of this book is the property of the copyright holder only. Mountain Arbor Press does not hold any ownership of the content of this book and is not liable in any way for the materials contained within. The views and opinions expressed in this book are the property of the Author/Copyright holder, and do not necessarily reflect those of Mountain Arbor Press/BookLogix.

Printed in the United States of America

♾ This paper meets the requirements of ANSI/NISO Z39.48-1992 (Permanence of Paper)

To contact the author, please visit jimdakin.com

051926

This book is dedicated to Karen Dakin, my lovely wife and soulmate of fifty-plus years, who has helped bring out the best in me, and helped me to see the light on many occasions. She has specifically shared and nurtured my interest in art. On our very first date we visited the Museum of Modern Art in New York City. Since then we have visited many art museums together, in the United States and abroad.

CONTENTS

INTRODUCTION

"Art is an aesthetic object. It is meant to be looked at and appreciated for its intrinsic value. Its special qualities set art apart, so that precious examples have often been placed away from everyday life – in museums, churches, or caves."

Janson 1986, page 9

The broad story of light deserves to be told in a widely accessible way. The history, applications, and science of light are fascinating, reaching across so many different narrow disciplines. Light shows up in most STEM disciplines to be sure, but also in history, philosophy, religion, art, and many others. It is nearly impossible to find the whole story condensed and interconnected in one place. This book tells the broad story in a unique way through art.

Art provides a great way to tell the story because all of the key ideas can be found in art. Artists and their works connect the ideas across many disciplines. Many artists display a visceral understanding of light phenomena. Art crosses cultures and is much less intimidating than equations, numbers, and even words.

My own connection with the story of light began in childhood and gradually developed into a career in the electric lighting industry. In writing a personal memoir for family and friends, I found myself using light as a connecting theme. This developed into my writing and publishing a textbook, *Wrestling with Light – History, Science and Applications*, that tells the story in a way intended for use in an interdisciplinary college-level course. In the fall of 2023, I taught a highly interdisciplinary honors seminar titled "Light and Color" at Appalachian State University in Boone, North Carolina. The course followed the textbook, and emphasized students choosing light-related topics of personal interest, researching them, and presenting to the class. Some art students were in the class.

These experiences stimulated this new way of telling the broad story of light, which in turn led me to write this book. Art captures most of the story of light, either directly or indirectly, and art has been around for millennia. Science underlies the story of light, although its full understanding has emerged only over the past 200 years. The internet and Wikipedia make the tiny pieces of this story instantly accessible to anyone who wishes to look further. These tools have blossomed over the past 20 years. Scholarly books have been available which allow one to dig much deeper in narrow areas, but I defy you, the reader, to find a source which captures the story of light as broadly as I do here.

Following the Introduction, the remainder of this book is organized into four parts:

> Part I introduces five key concepts involving the science of light in easily accessible language.

> Part II covers a very broad range of natural phenomena involving light.

> Part III then turns to human inventions involving light.

> Part IV concludes with a discussion of time in relationship to the light themes.

Throughout the book, I use art to help illustrate each topic discussed. The intent is to make each piece of artwork, along with its adjacent pages of text, a stand-alone story, henceforth called a "section." Many of the concepts are connected across sections, and often cross-referenced. There is also an extensive index to help make these connections.

In each of the sections I try to capture the essence of what could often be expanded into a whole book. References are provided for the reader who wants to learn more about a specific section or story. The intent here is to help the reader see the big picture by keeping the sections short and emphasizing the connections.

Thus, this book is *not* intended to be the definitive, scholarly text on any of its subjects. It *is* intended to make connections between all of its light-related subjects in a new and broadly accessible way.

Dates can be confusing. Specific dates are always either BCE (before the common era) or CE (common era). If the date is BCE, e.g. Aristotle (384-322 BCE), the "BCE" is *always* given. If the date is CE, e.g. Albert Einstein (1879-1955), the "CE" is sometimes omitted if it seems obvious. A third way of giving a general date is before the present. The Neolithic Revolution, for instance, began about 12,000 years ago. This approach makes sense for very early events for which there is no known specific date. In the Neolithic Revolution example there is no specific date because it took place at different times in different places around the world, there is no written record, and there is only imprecise archeological dating.

Art

Art is a uniquely human activity, defined as the expression or application of human creative skill and imagination. Here I will share visual forms, such as painting or sculpture, producing works to be appreciated primarily for their beauty or emotional power. A skilled artist can often capture an idea and convey it to the viewer much more effectively than words or any other form of communication. Furthermore, archeologists tell us that art has been around for at least 15,000 to 30,000 years based on cave paintings – much longer than written language, and unquestionably longer than settled science. (Some sources claim much earlier dates for certain cave paintings and for archaeological evidence of art. I am trying here to be conservative and still make the point.)

Artists had a visceral understanding of the properties of light long before science was able to codify those properties.

In our modern times, much art, including the earliest, is preserved in museums around the world and accessible to the public. To the extent possible, the museums document the provenance of each piece of art. In many cases the art can be seen online. In some cases, the museums make art available through open-access agreements. These agreements allow an author to include the online images in books without cost, but subject to certain citation rules that are helpful to both the museum and the reader.

The effectiveness of art at communicating ideas, and the easy access to so many images, provide a wonderful new opportunity for using art to tell a story, as is done here.

In some cases, the art in museums is primarily aesthetic, art for art's sake. In other cases, it is artifacts which are inherently practical, while often also being aesthetically pleasing. The line between the aesthetic and the practical is hard to draw. Examples of both are used in this book.

In selecting pieces of art to illustrate this book, I attempted to represent a variety of artforms, cultures, and time periods. Many museums offering open access are included. In some cases, I have chosen the earliest piece of art to illustrate a particular idea, to help establish the age of that idea. For instance, the 4,000-year-old Egyptian paint box that I display in the "Pigments" section of Part III shows that artists have been using different paint pigments for at least that long.

While the art illustrations included here help to tell the story, they do not do justice to the real thing -- the full scale, sometimes 3-D, art in the museums. If I show a particular image in the book that fascinates you, go to the museum and see the real thing! If you can't, go to the museum website using the information I provide, and see a better image!

Science

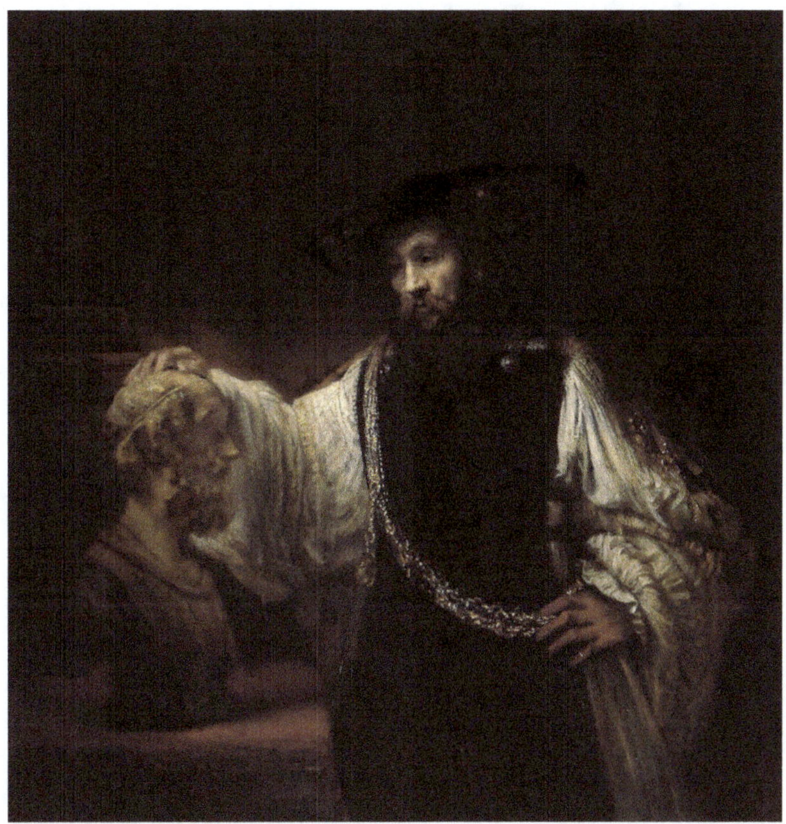

Science, which has been around for less than 3,000 years, is considerably younger than art at 15,000 to 30,000. The 1653 CE painting *Aristotle with a Bust of Homer* by Rembrandt (1606-1669) could not be more central to this book and story. The Greek philosopher Aristotle (384-322 BCE) plays a key role in the beginnings of science, with many of his writings touching light. It is fitting that the celebrated artist Rembrandt painted Aristotle 2,000 years after the latter's death.

The science that underlies the natural phenomena and human applications of light appearing in each of this book's examples is now well known. This science and a bit of its history are presented only in general terms. To be honest, the art, the light phenomena, and the inventions tell an interesting story all by themselves, even without the science! The reader wishing to learn more is directed not just to the cited reference books, but also to the internet and Wikipedia, as discussed next.

Internet/Wikipedia search term: science

Book reference: Dampier 1948

The 1653 painting *Aristotle with a Bust of Homer* by Rembrandt (Rembrandt van Rijn) (1606–1669), can be found at the Metropolitan Museum of Art, Purchase, special contributions and funds given or bequeathed by friends of the Museum, 1961, Accession Number 61.198. The image shown here is in the public domain under the Met's Open Access initiative.

Internet and Wikipedia

Considering art, science, and the internet, the latter is clearly the newest! In earlier times, when I wanted to learn more about something, I would go to a relevant book at home, or find one at a library. Encyclopedias were found in many homes, including mine, up through the 20th century CE. In our more modern times, I often want to learn more about something instantly. The computer and the internet now make this possible.

The books of earlier times and today were generally very reliable because they had gone through the vetting processes of editors, reviewers, publishers, and ultimately external review. The internet of today is generally less reliable because anyone can post anything, and much content is driven by advertising. Wikipedia may be somewhat more reliable because it has an inherent review process driven by stakeholders, and often provides references. Even so, Wikipedia can be confusing due to occurrence of more than one article on the same or closely related subjects. Wikipedia does provide links to related articles, which can be helpful. One needs to be careful when relying on the internet for quick answers.

Having said that, the remainder of this book provides suggested search terms for learning more about each specific topic. It also provides suggestions of more traditional books. Writing this book has relied heavily on the traditional books indicated herein, as well as on the internet and Wikipedia.

In four cases, when unable to find a suitable piece of art at one of the museums, I have used a public domain image from Wikipedia. The remaining 59 images come directly from museums.

PART I

THE SCIENCE OF LIGHT

"The vast and imposing structure of modern science is perhaps the greatest triumph of the human mind. But the story of its origin, its development and its achievements is one of the least known parts of history, and has hardly found its way into general literature."

Dampier 1948, preface

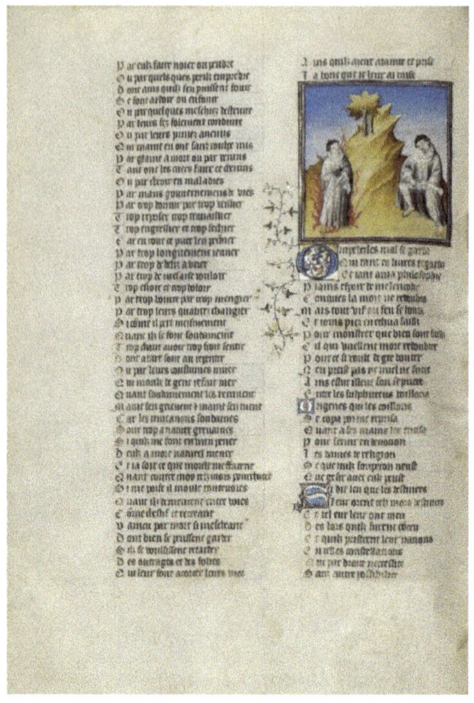

This illustration of *Empedocles Burning in the Crater of Aetna* by an unknown French artist highlights one of the earliest philosophers to speculate on vision. Without vision, we certainly would not know about light. Empedocles (circa 494 – 434 BCE) is credited with postulating that everything is made of four basic elements – earth, air, fire, and water. He also postulated the emission theory of vision, which I will get to in the "Eye and Vision" section of Part II.

Science has come a long way since Empedocles, but I respect that someone needed to get the ball rolling. In this case it was Empedocles, who influenced later Greek philosophy.

The basic science of light can get very complicated, as any optics or modern physics textbook quickly shows. A great source for learning the 3,000-year history of light science is the classic *A History of Science and its Relations with Philosophy and Religion* by William Dampier. In this book I will reduce it to some very simple basics – heat, waves, particles, color, and refraction. When the phenomenon is too abstract, I will show art that provides a metaphorical understanding, for example waves on water as a metaphor for light waves. The interested reader is always free to independently dig deeper.

Internet/Wikipedia search terms: Empedocles, light, science

Book references: Bragg 1936, Dampier 1948, Harris 2008, Hecht 2017, Zajonc 1993

The circa 1450 CE illustration of *Empedocles Burning in the Crater of Aetna* by an unknown artist can be found at the J. Paul Getty Museum, Object Number: Ms. Ludwig XV 7 (83.MR.177), fol. 107v. The image shown here is in the public domain under the Getty Museum's Creative Commons initiative.

3

Heat

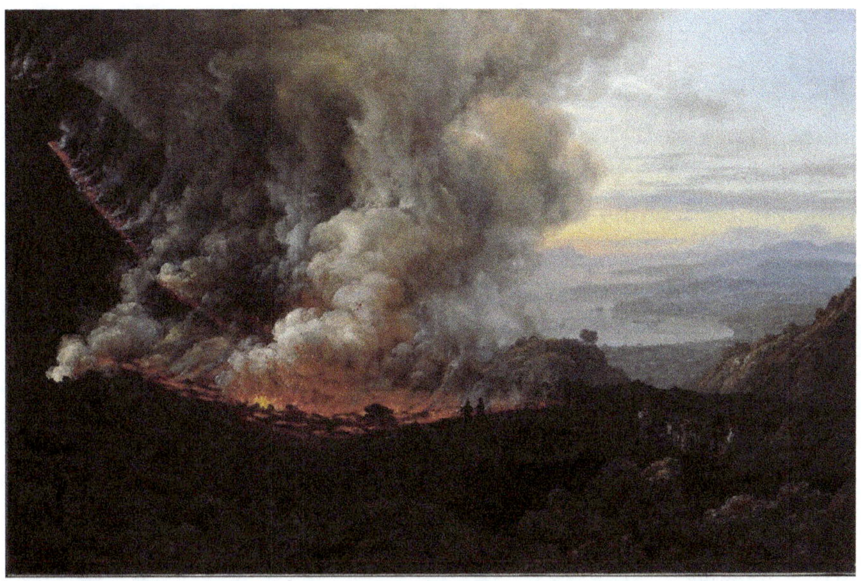

The 1824 CE painting *An Eruption of Vesuvius* by Johan Christian Dahl (1788-1857), a Norwegian artist, illustrates the well-known fact that things which are sufficiently hot give off light. This is seen in the hot cauldron of an erupting volcano, and in molten lava flowing from the volcano. It is also seen when an iron poker is put into a fire, and then brought back out. It is seen in the fire itself, as the hotter parts give off more light. It is seen in a conventional electric cook-top, whose burners glow as they become hot. It is seen in the Sun.

Scientists in the 1800s referred to this phenomenon as "blackbody radiation." An object, such as the poker, which seems inherently black when it is cold gives off radiation (light) when it gets hot. They learned that as the object gets hotter, the amount of light increases, and the light gets whiter. Max Planck (1858-1947) came up with a mathematical equation in 1901 which described black-body radiation perfectly, and continues to do so over a century later. Planck won the Nobel Prize for this in 1905. Planck's Law, the equation, contains a then-new constant now called Planck's Constant, which underlies what is now called quantum science. More about this in the "Particles" section of Part I.

In the "Aurora Borealis" and "Bioluminescence" sections in Part II of this book I will show you some "cold light" phenomena which have nothing to do with heat.

Internet/Wikipedia search terms: black-body radiation, Max Planck, Planck's Constant

Book references: Harris 2008, Dampier 1948, Zajonc 1993

The 1824 CE painting *An Eruption of Vesuvius* by Johan Christian Dahl (1788–1857) can be found at the Metropolitan Museum of Art, Gift of Christen Sveaas, in celebration of the Museum's 150th Anniversary, 2019, Accession Number 2019.167.1. The image shown here is in the public domain under the Met's Open Access initiative.

Waves

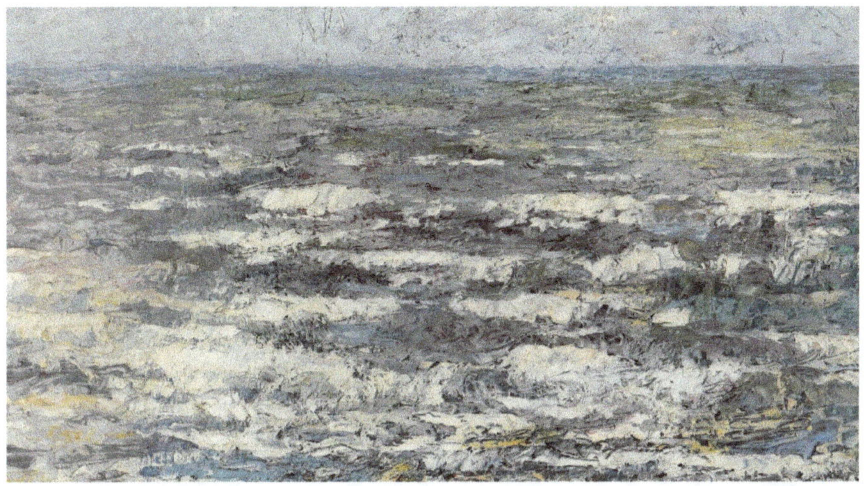

So… what *is* light? Philosophers and scientists have speculated on this topic for over 2,000 years.

The 1887 painting *The Sea* by the Dutch artist Jan Toorop (1858-1928) shows waves approaching shore in the ocean. Its museum inscription reads, "Jan Toorop made this seascape in Katwijk, where he was living in 1887. It is painted partly with a paintbrush and partly with a palette knife, as can be seen in the flat strokes. Through this technique, he succeeded in suggesting the effect of the waves breaking on the seashore in a realistic, almost tangible way. But if you look more closely, you can see a fantastic medley of colors."

Waves on water were a familiar phenomenon from very early on. It was obvious that waves could be excited, could travel from one point to another, and could make things happen when they reached shore. The waves are not the water; they travel across the water.

From the 1600s on, natural philosophers such as Christiaan Huygens (1629-1695) conjectured that light consists of analogous waves traveling through an invisible omnipresent substance called "aether." This wave theory of light gained credibility when Thomas Young (1773-1829) demonstrated the "diffraction" of light, in which waves from different sources collide to form "interference" patterns. The patterns allow determination of the "wavelength" of light, analogous to the distance between the crests of waves on water. (The wavelength of visible light is much, much smaller than the diameter of a human hair.)

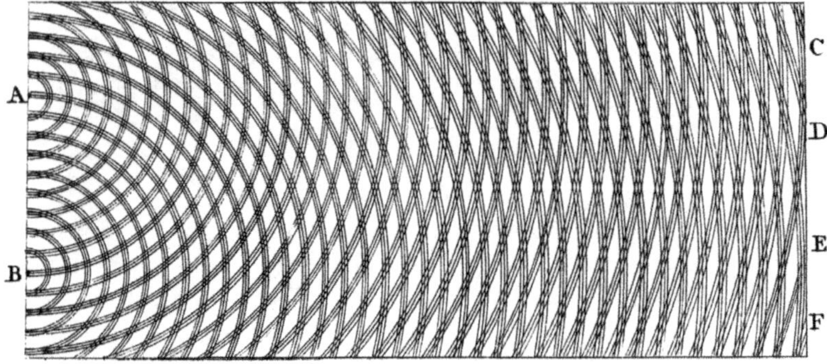

This 1803 drawing by Thomas Young shows patterns formed when waves from two separate point sources of light, A and B, interfere with each other at angles C, D, E and F. Similar diffraction phenomena can be seen with water waves in a ripple tank, as can readily be found through an internet search.

The wave explanation of light was thought to have won the day in 1865, when James Clerk Maxwell (1831-1879) presented some mathematical equations with which he connected electricity and magnetism. These equations miraculously predicted waves, and the predicted waves had exactly the same velocity as had been measured for the speed of light. Maxwell's Equations accounted for other properties of light as well, such as polarization and refraction. Maxwell's Equations are now central to what is taught to STEM students about electricity, magnetism, and light.

Internet/Wikipedia search terms: Huygens, interference, light, Maxwell (James Clerk), Maxwell's Equations, polarization, ripple tank interference, Young (Thomas)

Book references: Harris 2008, Dampier 1948, Zajonc 1993

The 1887 CE drawing *The Sea* by Jan Toorop (1858-1928) can be found at the Rijksmuseum, Gift of I. Lohr, Basel, Object Number: SK-A-4226. The image shown here is in the public domain under the Rijksmuseum's Creative Commons program.

The 1803 Young drawing is taken from Wikipedia. Wikipedia states, "it is in the public domain in its country of origin and other countries and areas where the copyright term is the author's life plus 70 years or fewer."

Particles

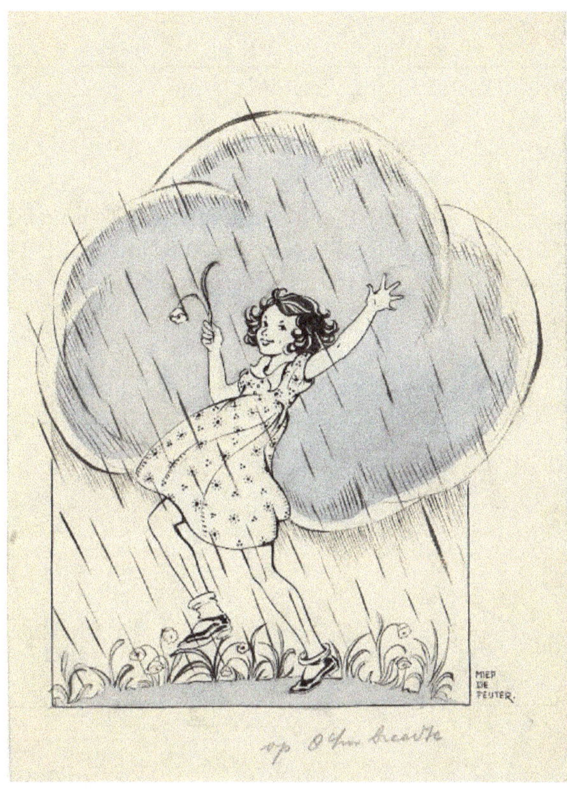

The circa 1941 CE drawing *Dancing in the Rain* by artist Miep de Feijter (born 1908) also involves water, this time in the form of rain drops. Rain drops were as familiar as waves on water to scientists of the past. Isaac Newton (1642-1726 CE) viewed light as particles, not waves. This could explain, for instance, the well-established fact that light inherently travels in straight lines, much like the raindrops in the drawing. The particle theory also helped explain Newton's theory of color, to be discussed further in the next section. Whether light is particles or waves remained an open question long after the time of Huygens and Newton.

Later, Albert Einstein (1879-1955) interpreted Planck's Law describing black-body radiation as requiring light to be "quantized" into particles, later called "photons." Each photon had a unique energy associated with its wavelength by Planck's

Constant. This particle affirmation, arguably, enhanced Newton's already high stature.

Starting about 100 years ago, in modern quantum theory, light has come to be viewed as particles and waves at the same time, sometimes behaving more like the former and sometimes the latter.

Internet/Wikipedia search terms: Einstein, light, Newton, photon

Book references: Harris 2008, Dampier 1948, Zajonc 1993

The ~1941 CE drawing *Dancing in the Rain* by Miep de Feijter (born 1908) can be found at the Rijksmuseum, Gift of Uitgeverij L.J. Veen, Object Number: RP-T-2015-41-389. The image shown here is in the public domain under the Rijksmuseum's Creative Commons program.

Rainbow and Color

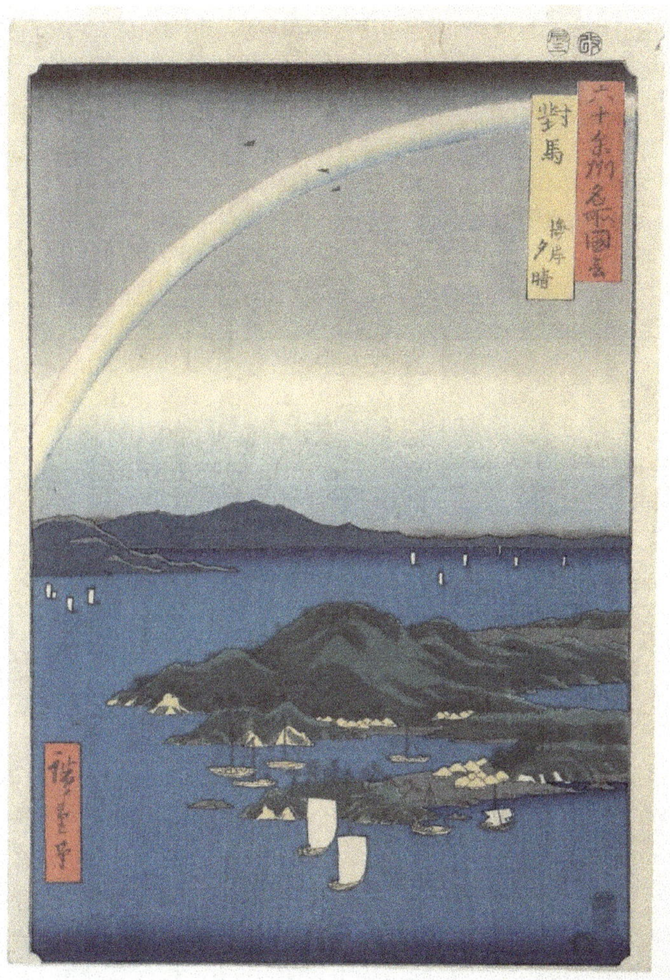

The 1856 woodblock print titled Tsushima Coast Oil Barre by
Japanese artist Utagawa Hiroshige (1797-1858) highlights a rainbow over a harbor. The rainbow plays a central role in our scientific understanding of color. Specifically, the rainbow contains

the primary colors – red, yellow, green and blue when coming inward from the outside arc of the primary rainbow. Isaac Newton (1642-1726) is credited with developing a scientific understanding of color based upon the primary colors. He showed that he could separate white sunlight to form the primary colors, then re-combine those primary colors to form white. In Newton's view, the light of each primary color is associated with particles of light having that color. In Young's view, each primary color is associated with a specific wavelength – blue has the shortest wavelength of the primary colors, red has the longest. Both views are considered scientifically valid today.

	Primary Color	Wave View (Huygens… Maxwell): **Wavelength**	Particle View (Newton… Einstein): **Photon Energy**
White	Red	longest	lowest
	Yellow	longer	lower
	Green	shorter	higher
	Blue	shortest	highest

In the world of color science and color mixing, there are two basic concepts – additive mixing and subtractive mixing. Adding red and blue together makes purple. Subtracting yellow and green from white leaves red and blue, which also makes purple. These terms are somewhat simplistic because white, for instance, could be made with a single wavelength each in the red, yellow, green, and blue parts of the spectrum, in proper proportions. It could also be "full spectrum" white, with *all* the wavelengths included in proper amounts according to Planck's Law, and as seen in the rainbow.

An object, such as a painting, illuminated with full spectrum white is more likely to reveal its own true colors. This is why artists prefer to work under full spectrum illumination and museums prefer to display artwork under full spectrum illumination. Sunlight comes very close to having a full spectrum; many electric lighting sources fall short to some degree, trading a somewhat less than full spectrum for energy efficiency.

I will say more about the science of the rainbow in the Part II "Reflection" section. It must also be said that the rainbow has had, and continues to have, a huge role in culture. Zajonc writes, "With the dawn of a sentient humanity, the spectral arc of the heavens we call the rainbow began its enchantment of the human mind. It has been a source of wonder, myth, superstition…" Zajonc goes on to follow the rainbow through the ancient Semitic peoples, Genesis, Homer, and ancient cultures worldwide. The rainbow remains a cultural metaphor today. [Zajonc 1993, p. 164]

Internet/Wikipedia search terms: light, color, Isaac Newton, rainbow

Book references: Hecht 2017, Dampier 1948, Waldman 1983, Zajonc 1993

The 1856 CE woodblock print *Tsushima Coast Oil Barre* by artist Utagawa Hiroshige (1797–1858) can be found at the Metropolitan Museum of Art, Purchase, Joseph Pultizer Bequest, 1918, Accession Number JP592. The image shown here is in the public domain under the Met's Open Access initiative.

Refraction

The 1870 CE painting *A Road in Louveciennes* by artist Auguste Renoir (1841-1919) shows a road that is not straight. The road meanders in response to subtle variations in the local terrain, avoiding hills, for instance. If this road were on a flat prairie, it would probably be straight.

In the initial development of optics by Euclid (born ~325 BCE), light was viewed as traveling in straight lines -- like the straight road on the prairie envisioned in the preceding paragraph, or like the raindrops in the earlier section on "Particles."

It took close to 2,000 years after Euclid for science to fully understand that the straight lines only occur when light is traveling through a transparent medium with uniform properties, like uniform temperature air, water, or glass.

When the medium does not have uniform properties, or when the light passes between two media with different properties, the light may bend. Maxwell's Equations, presented in 1865 and mentioned earlier in the "Waves" section, can account for this bending. The bending or turning of the light in response to the varying material properties is analogous to the bending of the road in response to the terrain in Renoir's painting.

This bending phenomenon, called refraction, will come up again in the "Mirage and Refraction" and "Sunset" sections of Part II, and the "Lenses" section of Part III.

Internet/Wikipedia search term: refraction

Book references: Hecht 2017, Dampier 1948, Waldman 1983, Zajonc 1993

The 1870 CE painting *A Road in Louveciennes* by artist Auguste Renoir (1841-1919) can be found at the Metropolitan Museum of Art, The Lesley and Emma Sheafer Collection, Bequest of Emma A. Sheafer, 1973, Accession Number 1974.356.32. The image shown here is in the public domain under the Met's Open Access initiative.

PART II

NATURAL PHENOMENA

Genesis 1

1 In the beginning God created the heaven and the earth.

2 And the earth was without form, and void; and darkness was upon the face of the deep. And the Spirit of God moved upon the face of the waters.

3 And God said, Let there be light: and there was light.

4 And God saw the light, that it was good: and God divided the light from the darkness.

5 And God called the light Day, and the darkness he called Night. And the evening and the morning were the first day.

King James Bible

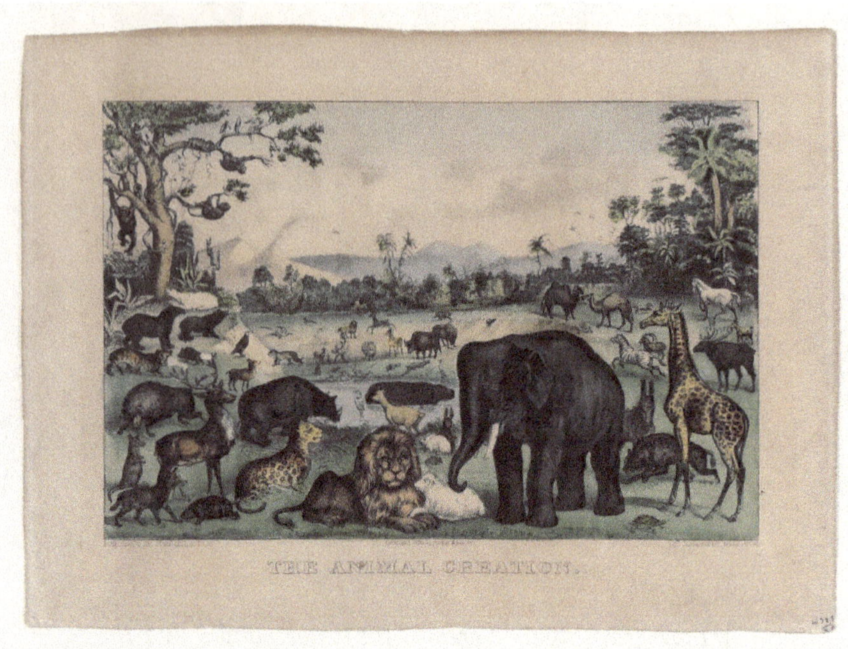

This hand-colored lithograph titled *The Animal Creation* was published by Currier & Ives in 1875. It envisions a world where "wild and domesticate animals from the four continents gather here peacefully near a watering hole" and humans are not around to cause trouble. Consider the Biblical creation account of Genesis and the Garden of Eden before God created man.

A great many phenomena involving light are evident in the natural world, many as obvious to plants and animals in their own ways as to humans. Our human ancestors were presumably familiar with these phenomena long before they became homo sapiens half a million years ago, before they started capturing them in written language or trying to explain them with science.

Science now gives us the following scenario:

~ 14 billion years ago – the "Big Bang" of creation,

~ 5 billion years ago – our Sun and planets formed,

~ 4 billion years ago – first life on our Earth,

~ 400 million years ago – first uncontrolled fire, and

~ 300,000 years ago – first homo sapiens.

Internet/Wikipedia search terms: creation, evolution, nature

Book reference: (none)

The 1875 CE hand-colored lithograph titled The Animal Creation published by Currier & Ives (1857–1907) can be found at the Metropolitan Museum of Art, Bequest of Adele S. Colgate, 1962, Accession Number 63.550.338. The image shown here is in the public domain under the Met's Open Access initiative.

Eye and Vision

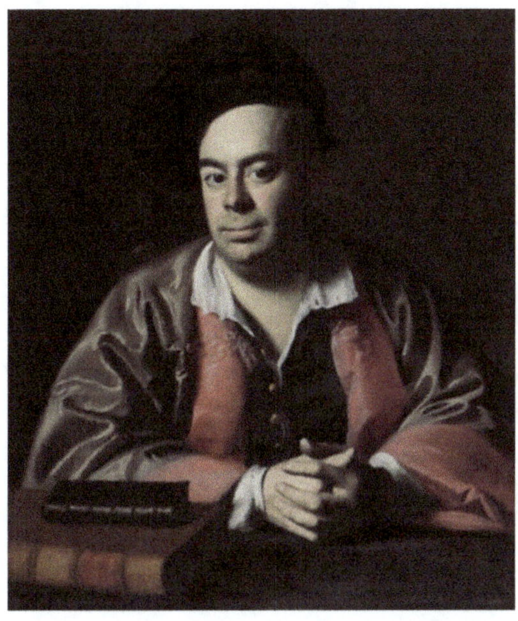

A good natural phenomenon to start Part II with is the eye and vision. Eyes and vision enable us to know about light.

The painting of *Nathaniel Hurd*, circa 1765 CE, is by John Singleton Copley (1738–1815). Hurd seems to be looking right at you, the viewer. Credit Copley's keen eye and artistic talent for capturing this so well!

Our eyes are amazing, providing perhaps the most vivid and essential of our five senses for those of us lucky to have good eyesight. Eyes have been around for quite a while. Evolutionary biology tells us that the first eyes appeared in much lower animals roughly 500 million years ago. Close to 3,000 years ago, Empedocles (circa 494–434 BCE) is credited as the first to speculate as to how the eye actually works. In Empedocles' theory of earth, air, fire, and water, Aphrodite lit the fire in the eye, which then reaches out and comes back with what the eye sees.

Leonardo da Vinci (1452-1519 CE) rejected Empedocles' "emission theory" of vision, and said that the eye works like a camera obscura, Latin for dark room, a Roman era invention for which the modern camera is named. (Part III contains a "Camera Obscura" section.) Leonardo was particularly concerned that the lens in the eye would make an upside-down image on the retina. Science now tells us that the brain somehow sorts that all out and things appear right side up. Today, modern ophthalmology can deal quite effectively with lots of different vision defects, helping many of us see better. What an amazing story!

The lens in the eye provides an example of refraction, one of the best in nature. The "Lens" section in Part III will address this in greater detail.

Internet/Wikipedia search terms: eye, vision

Book references: Ayscough 1752, Clair 2017, Gross 2002, Russell 2017, Waldman 1983

The ~1765 CE painting of *Nathaniel Hurd* by John Singleton Copley (1738–1815) can be found at the Cleveland Museum of Art, Gift of the John Huntington Art and Polytechnic Trust, Accession Number 1915.534. The image shown here is in the public domain under the CMA's Open Access initiative.

Sun

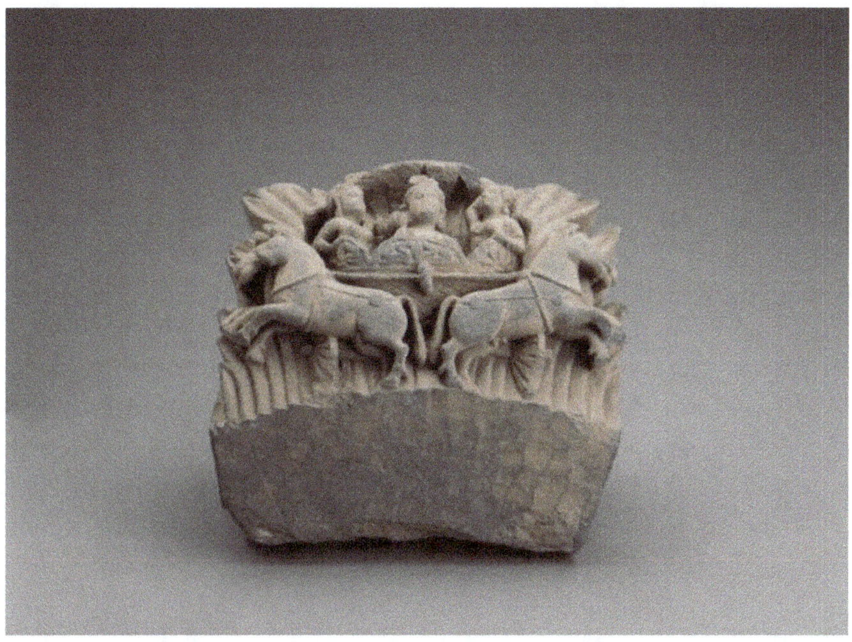

The Sun has been the primary source of light and heat on Earth for as long as there has been life. The day-night cycle provided by the Sun helps define life. Moving away from the Equator, the Sun defines the seasons. It is no wonder that the Sun plays a role in so many early religions and their associated art. Here I show a stone carving of *Surya, the Hindu Sun God*, dated to be early 200s CE.

Whether you choose the story of science, or any of the creation myths from around the world, the Sun is a big deal.

Science now tells us that the Sun behaves very much like a black-body radiator, whose surface temperature is ~5800 degrees Kelvin. According to Planck's Law, this puts the peak light from the Sun right at the middle of the human eye sensitivity curve. This can't be a coincidence, whether you believe in science or any of the creation myths. This maximizes our ability to see, whether in broad daylight or by sunlight bouncing off the Moon at night.

The 1570s CE painting on the next page is by French artist Antoine Caron (1521-1599). It is titled *Dionysius the Areopagite Converting the Pagan Philosophers*. It's museum inscription reads, "In 1571 a dramatic solar eclipse occurred: this event probably served as the subject of this painting by Antoine Caron. He painted it at the court of Catherine de Medici, queen of France, who, like many rulers of the time, was extremely superstitious and fascinated by astronomical phenomena, often seeing eclipses and natural disasters as foreboding omens."

"In the painting, astronomers gather in a town square beneath the shadowed sun. A bearded Greek philosopher in the foreground looks at the sky and points to an armillary sphere on the ground. Next to him, the central figure, Dionysius the Areopagite, holds a book, points to the sky, and looks at the celestial globe carried by the figure running up the steps at the right. Dionysius preaches the Christian message of salvation to pagan Greek philosophers. A putto, seated on the steps between a square and straight edge, writes on a tablet, recording the event."

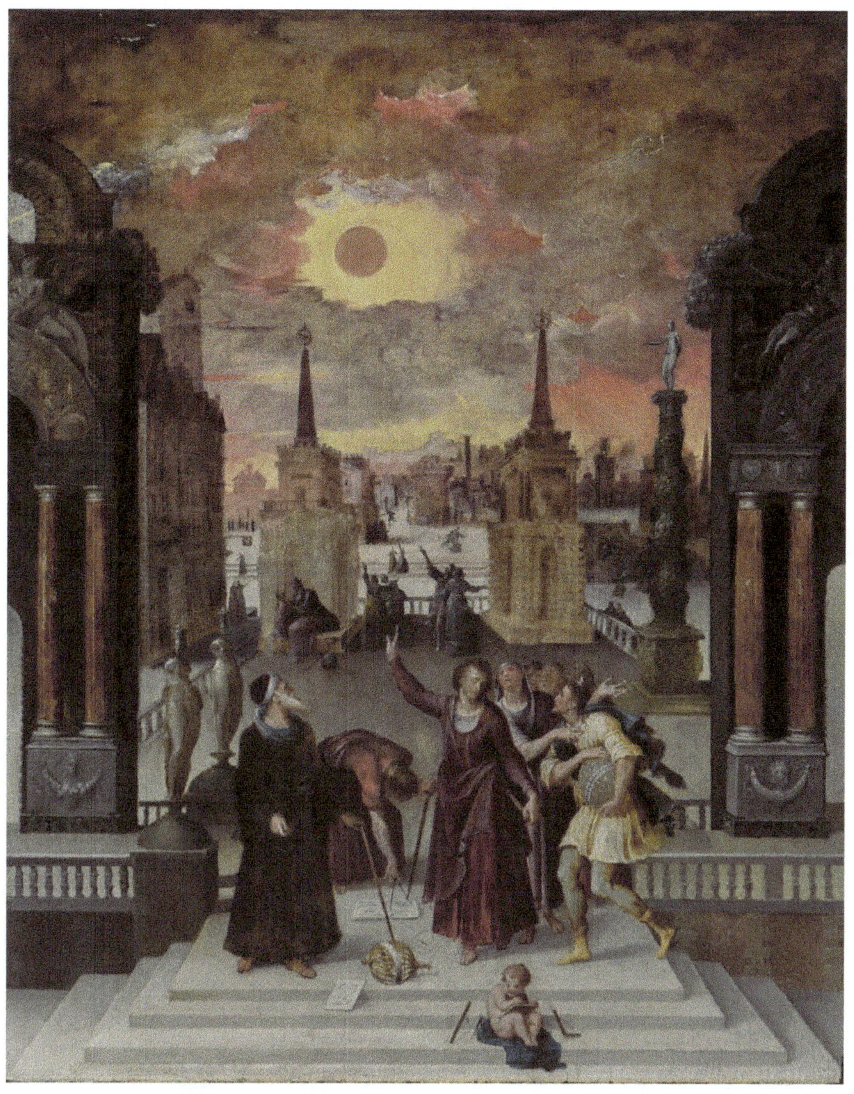

The Sun has played a key role in the evolution of life on Earth. It has been important throughout human history. It has been a source of mystery and wonder to our ancestors, especially before modern science largely de-mystified so many of its related phenomena. Almost all the remainder of Part II deals with natural phenomena related to the Sun directly or indirectly. The "Religion" section in Part III has more about the Sun.

Internet/Wikipedia search terms: sun, creation, eclipse, evolution, earth, homo sapiens, Surya

Book references: Gross 2002, Sproul 1979, Tyson 2017

The circa 200 CE stone carving of *Surya, the sun god* by an unknown Indian artist can be found at the Indianapolis Museum of Art at Newfields, Gift of Mr. and Mrs. Charles B. Miller, Accession Number 74.629. The image shown here is in the public domain under the museum's Open Access initiative.

The 1570s CE painting *Dionysius the Areopagite Converting the Pagan Philosophers* by Antoine Caron (1521-1599) can be found at the J. Paul Getty Museum, Object Number: 85.PB.117. The image shown here is in the public domain under the Getty Museum's Creative Commons initiative.

Moon

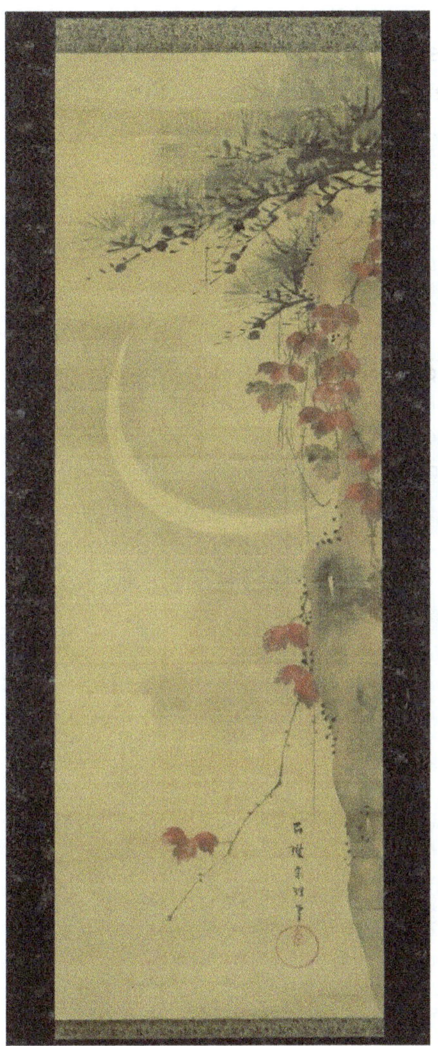

This hanging scroll titled *Moon, Pine and Maple* was made of ink, colors and gold on silk by Japanese artist Katsushika Hokusai somewhere in the period 1764-80.

The Moon has played a much less significant role in life on Earth than the Sun, mostly providing a bit of light at night to help nocturnal animals see. There are certain sea turtles that lay their eggs on the beach only at the full Moon. The Moon is also responsible for the oceanic tides due to its gravitational effects.

The Moon enchanted our ancestors with its ability to change shape, or phase, from new to quarter to half to full and back. (We now know from science how the Moon's orbit causes these shapes.) These shape phenomena have played a role in mythology and culture. In earlier times, the full Moon in the fall was called a harvest moon because it helped farmers to see at night as they were bringing in crops. Some viewed moonlight as different than sunlight. Now we know the former is just a reflection of the latter.

The Moon plays a key role in lunar and solar eclipses. In the former case the Earth shadows the Moon, and in the latter case the Moon shadows the Earth. Just imagine how terrifying a solar eclipse, like the one mentioned in the previous Sun section, must have been to someone who worshipped the Sun and was not expecting the eclipse. Now science lets us anticipate future eclipses with mathematical precision. So much of the Moon's mystery is now gone.

Internet/Wikipedia search term: moon

Book references: Gross 2002, Sproul 1979, Tyson 2017

The circa 1770 CE hanging scroll titled *Moon, Pine and Maple* by Katsushika Hokusai (active 1764-1780) can be found at the Art Institute of Chicago, Gift of Mr. and Mrs. Harold G. Henderson, Reference Number 1965.920. The image shown here is in the public domain under the museum's Creative Commons program.

Stars

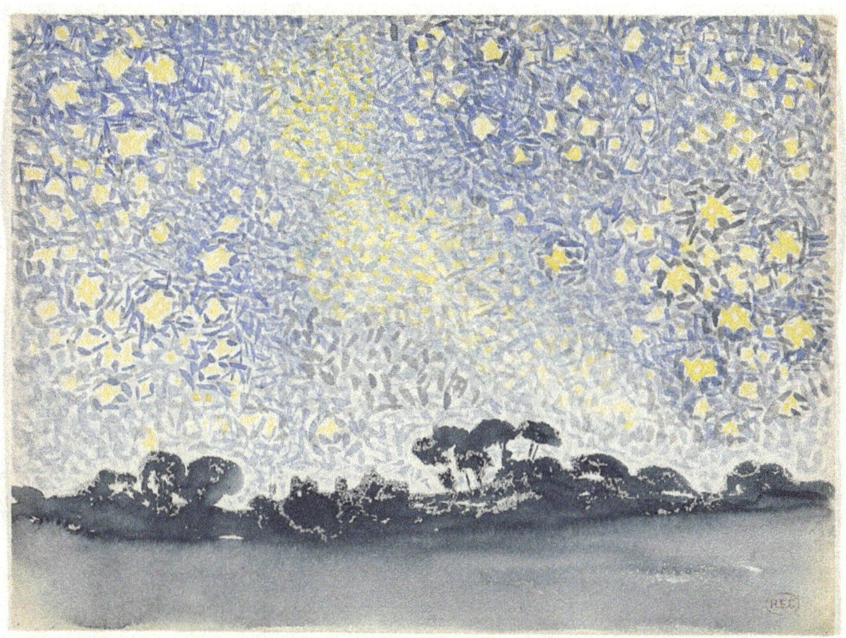

The stars are plainly visible on a clear night, but have played a less significant role in nature here on Earth than did the Sun or the Moon. The circa 1905 CE painting *Landscape with Stars* by artist Henri-Edmond Cross (1856-1910) makes them really pop out. Indeed they do if you can find the proper viewing conditions today. There is even a hint of the Milky Way in the painting.

While stars may have played little role in nature, they have unquestionably made an important contribution to science. The pre-science of astrology and early religions attached importance to the stars, and to the constellations - the consistent patterns the stars make from night to night. In the northern hemisphere, the

North Star, Polaris, stays at the same place night after night and season after season. The rest of the constellations appear to revolve around it in the course of a year.

Progressions in science and the field of astronomy have told us that the stars which can be seen with naked eyes are objects similar to our Sun. They are just much farther away, in our own galaxy, the Milky Way. Telescopes have helped astronomers find other galaxies, generally too far away to see with the naked eye, each with its own stars. Part III has a "Telescope" section with more about this important instrument.

Internet/Wikipedia search terms: star, astrology, astronomy

Book references: Tyson 2017, Dampier 1948

The circa 1905-1908 CE painting *Landscape with Stars* by artist Henri-Edmond Cross (Henri-Edmond Delacroix) (1856–1910) can be found at the Metropolitan Museum of Art, Robert Lehman Collection, 1975, Accession Number 1975.1.592. The image shown here is in the public domain under the Met's Open Access initiative.

Planets

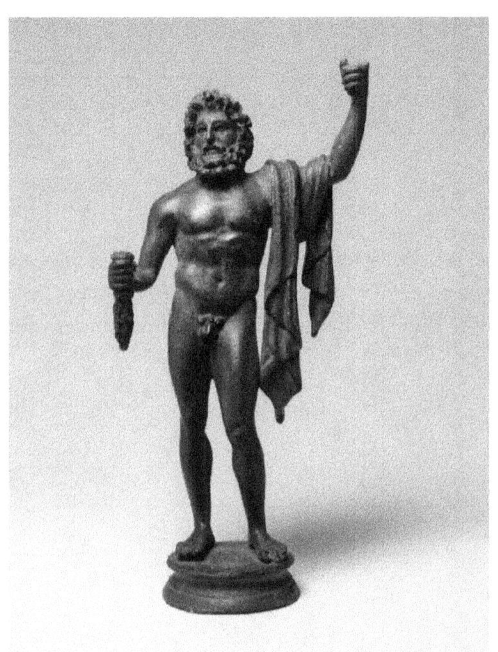

The planets were more exciting in astrology than the stars because they were fewer, and moved from night to night relative to the fixed stars. They were called "wandering stars." They sometimes even formed conjunctions with one another, to which ancient people assigned significance. The planets even became gods, as exemplified by this bronze statue of the Roman god *Jupiter* from the late 1st century CE.

The planets played a huge role in the development of modern science. Nicolaus Copernicus (1473-1543 CE) made the then shocking suggestion that the planets circle the Sun, not the Earth. Equally shocking, our Earth was just another planet! Johannes Kepler (1571-1630 CE) figured out that their orbits were mathematical ellipses. Isaac Newton (1643-1726 CE) invented calculus and the laws of motion to explain those ellipses. Add Albert Einstein (1879-1955) to the list, as his general theory of relativity improved upon Newton's work.

The story gets even better. Many of the planets were found to have moons circling them, most notably Jupiter. Ole Romer

(1644-1710 CE) found a way to measure the speed of light by carefully tracking and timing the orbit of a moon of Jupiter as our planet Earth circled the Sun. This provided the first measurement of the speed of light and came reasonably close to the now accepted value, consistent with Maxwell's Equations. The moons of Jupiter got Galileo Galilei (1564-1642 CE) into trouble, as I will tell about in the "Telescope" section of Part III.

Internet/Wikipedia search terms: planet, Copernican Revolution, moon, astrology, speed of light, astronomy

Book references: Tyson 2017, Dampier 1948

The late 1st century CE bronze statue of *Jupiter* by an unknown Roman artist can be found at the Metropolitan Museum of Art, Rogers Fund, 1922, Accession Number 22.139.37. The image shown here is in the public domain under the Met's Open Access initiative.

Aurora Borealis

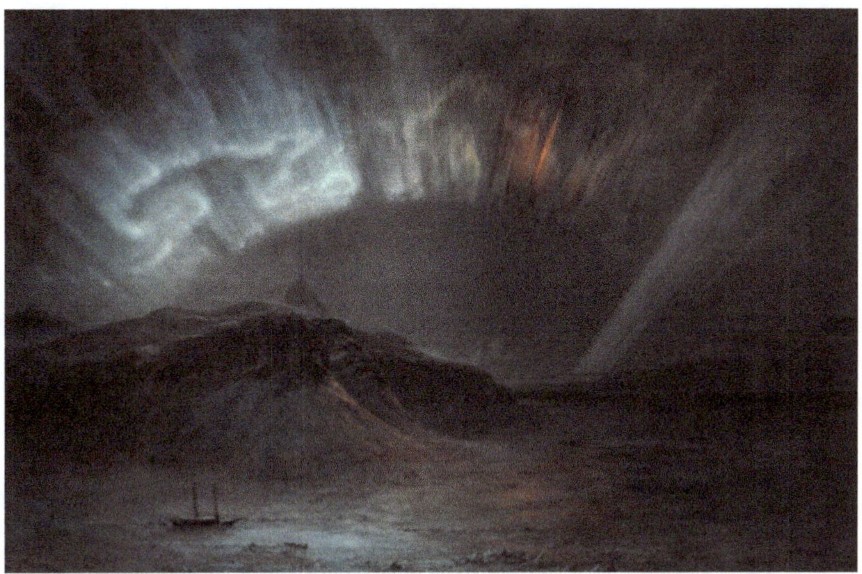

The 1865 painting by Frederick Edwin Church (1826-1900) titled *Aurora Borealis* highlights spectacular phenomena seen most often near the poles at night. The aurora borealis, also referred to as the northern lights or southern lights, are caused by interaction of solar wind with the Earth's magnetic field and upper atmosphere. The phenomenon is most intense and most readily visible near the poles where the magnetic fields are strongest. It is also most intense when there is sunspot activity contributing lots of charged electrons and protons to the solar wind. While aurora borealis can be seen most readily close to the poles, it has also been seen rarely in southern Europe and the southern US.

Unlike the light from the Sun and stars, which is created by heat, the light from aurora borealis comes from a cold light mechanism having nothing to do with heat. The aurora borealis, again unlike the Sun and the stars, appears broad and ethereal.

While a full scientific understanding of aurora borealis has come only in the past century, our ancestors knew about it for a very long time. Aristotle (384-322 BCE) wrote about aurora borealis, for example. The ancients were much more aware of the stars, planets, and aurora borealis than people today because the absence of light pollution made these phenomena more readily visible until around 200 years ago.

Internet/Wikipedia search terms: aurora borealis

Book reference: Harvey 2005

The 1865 painting *Aurora Borealis* by Frederic Edwin Church (1826-1900) can be found at the Smithsonian American Art Museum, Gift of Eleanor Blodgett, Accession Number 1911.4.1. The Smithsonian American Art Museum identifies this image as free to use.

Lightning

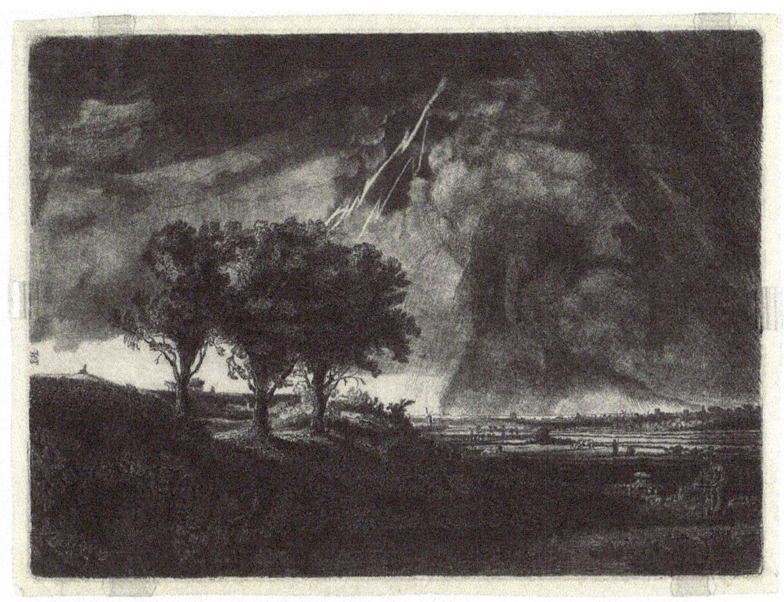

The 1758 etching by Captain William E. Baillie (1723–1810) titled *The Three Trees, after Rembrandt* shows a lightning strike, familiar now to almost anyone who has been or looked outdoors during a thunderstorm. Lighting has been around for ~5 billion years, as long as the Earth has had an atmosphere. Lightning and volcanic activity are the earliest terrestrial sources of light. Lightning started lighting natural fires about 400 million years ago, once photosynthesis had enabled oxygen to fill the atmosphere, and there were enough plants such as trees and grass to provide fuel. There is more to come in the sections on plants and fire.

Another important chapter in the role of lighting occurs later with Benjamin Franklin (1706-1790). Franklin did his famous experiment of flying a kite in a thunderstorm, showing that lightning is electrical in nature. This pretty quickly led to our understanding that electricity flowing through a lighting stroke is heating the local air so hot as to emit light. This brings us back to the Part I section on Heat, and takes us forward to the Part III section on modern Electric Lighting. The 1876 Currier & Ives lithograph below depicts Franklin's historic experiment.

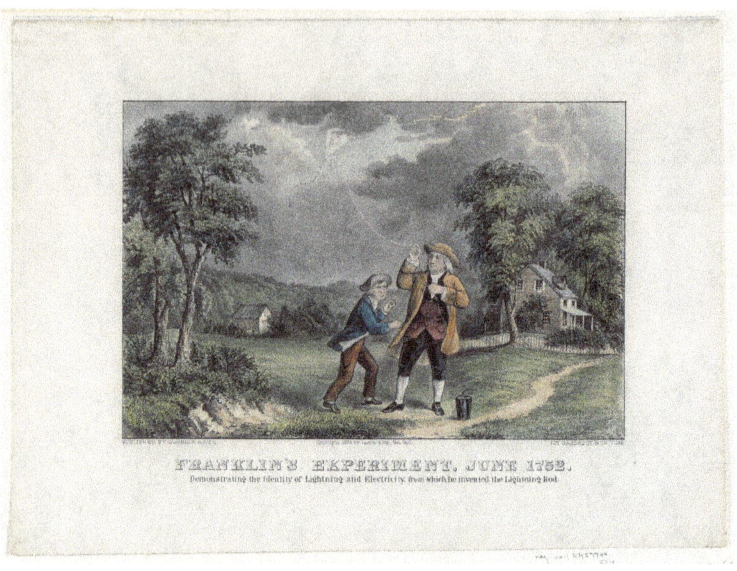

Internet/Wikipedia search terms: lightning, Benjamin Franklin

Book reference: Dampier 1948, Pyne 2019, Zajonc 1993

The 1758 etching titled *The Three Trees, after Rembrandt* is by artist Captain William E. Baillie (Irish, Kilbride, County Carlow 1723–1810 London) after Rembrandt (Rembrandt van Rijn) (Dutch, Leiden 1606–1669 Amsterdam). It can be found at the Metropolitan Museum of Art, Gift of Bonnie and Manuel Schonhorn, 2011, Accession Number 2011.521.4. The image shown here is in the public domain under the Met's Open Access initiative.

The 1876 hand colored lithograph titled *Franklin's Experiment, June 1752 – Demonstrating the identity of Lightning and Electricity, from which he invented the Lightning Rod* is from Currier & Ives (American, active New York, 1857–1907) and can be found at the Metropolitan Museum of Art, Bequest of A. S. Colgate. 1962, Object Number: 63.550.329. The image shown here is in the public domain under the Met's Open Access initiative.

Shadow

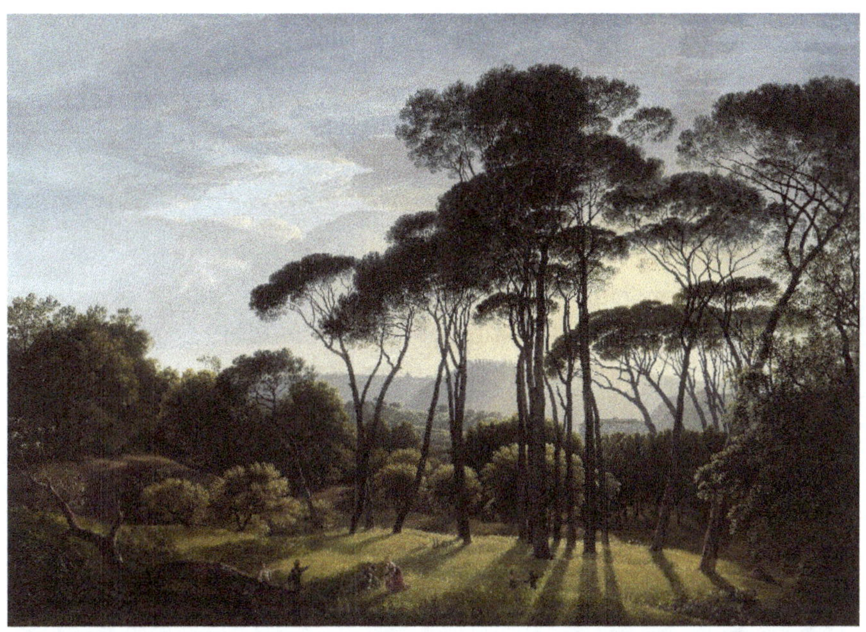

The painting *Italian Landscape with Umbrella Pines* by Hendrik Voogd (1768-1839) illustrates the familiar phenomenon of shadow. When the light comes from a single place, the light source is called a point source. Light radiates outward in straight lines, and objects in the light's path cast shadows wherever the light ultimately lands. The sharper the point source, the sharper the shadows. The distant Sun on a clear day is pretty close to being a point source, and its shadows are sharp enough, as in this painting. Good artists understand shadows very well and get them right.

Shadows provide one of the clearest pieces of evidence that light travels in straight lines. This must have been obvious to our human ancestors long before recorded history. For this reason, straight lines were central to Euclid's (born ~325 BCE) understanding of optics, which was based on geometry and straight lines. Curiously, the reference books cited below covering Euclid, optics, and art do not even index the word *shadow*! Perhaps it is too obvious to deserve indexing. Wikipedia, however, does have an entry for *shadow*.

In the years following Euclid, it gradually became clear in the development of science that light only travels in straight lines in special cases -- transparent materials with uniform optical properties, such as vacuum, air, water, or glass. Light bends as it passes between two such materials with different properties. It took quite a while for science and optics to properly sort this out. More about this in the "Refraction," "Mirage and Refraction," and "Lens" sections of Parts I, II, and III respectively.

Internet/Wikipedia search terms: shadow, optics, Euclid

Book references: Dampier 1948, Hecht 2017, Janson 1986, Zajonc 1993

The 1807 CE painting *Italian Landscape with Umbrella Pines* by artist Hendrik Voogd (1768-1839) can be found at the Rijksmuseum, purchase 1976, Object Number: SK-A-4688. The image shown here is in the public domain under the Rijksmuseum's Creative Commons program.

Reflection and Rainbow

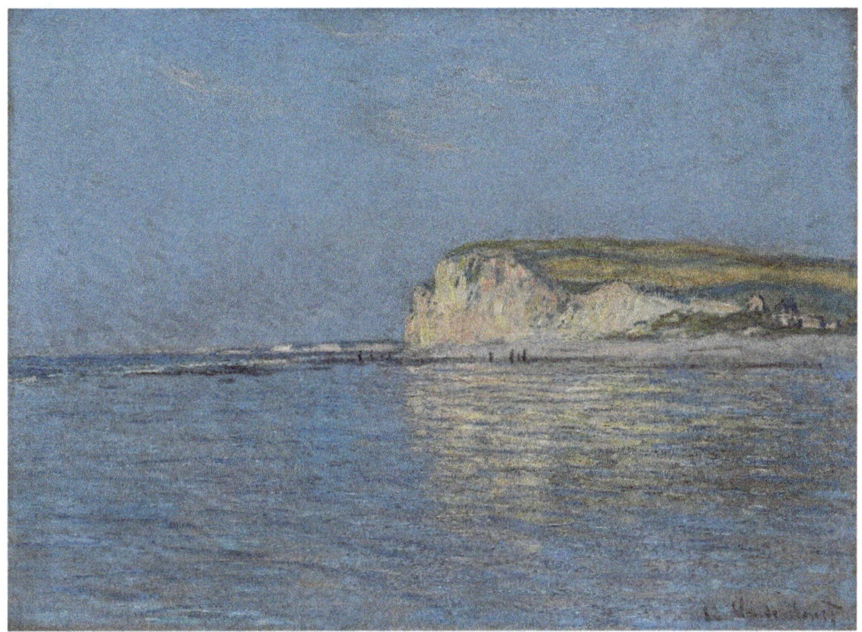

The 1882 CE painting *Low Tide at Pourville* by Claude Monet (1840-1926) highlights the reflection of the distant cliff. Still water would produce a sharper reflection, but an artist like Monet captures beauty through the ripples.

Reflection must have been noticed by our early ancestors, and even by animals as they traveled near or even drank from still water. In Greek mythology, Narcissus fell in love with his own reflection.

Reflection played a key role in the early development of optics. Euclid (born ~325 BCE) is credited with establishing the laws of reflection in association with geometry, laws which stand to this day in modern science.

Reflection and refraction both play key roles in the rainbow phenomenon, whose beauty our ancient ancestors surely noticed with delight. Rainbows are formed by droplets of water in the atmosphere. The droplets are in front of the observer while the Sun is behind. Light from the Sun enters a droplet, where it bends slightly, reflects off the back surface of the droplet, and then bends again coming back out. The different primary colors of light bend (refract) by slightly different angles to create the rainbow effect. Aristotle (384-322 BCE) wrote about the rainbow, but its mechanism was not fully understood until 2,000 years later by Isaac Newton (1624-1726 CE). I recommend the Wikipedia article to the reader who wants to really see how this works.

Reflection and refraction are closely interrelated in terms of Maxwell's Equations and modern science, where the distinction blurs in cases like the mirage phenomena described in the next section.

Internet/Wikipedia search terms: reflection, optics, rainbow

Book references: Dampier 1948, Hecht 2017, Zajonc 1993

The 1882 CE painting *Low Tide at Pourville, near Dieppeby* by Claude Monet (1840-1926) can be found at the Cleveland Museum of Art, Gift of Mrs. Henry White Cannon, Accession Number 1947.196. The image shown here is in the public domain under the CMA's Open Access initiative.

Mirage and Refraction

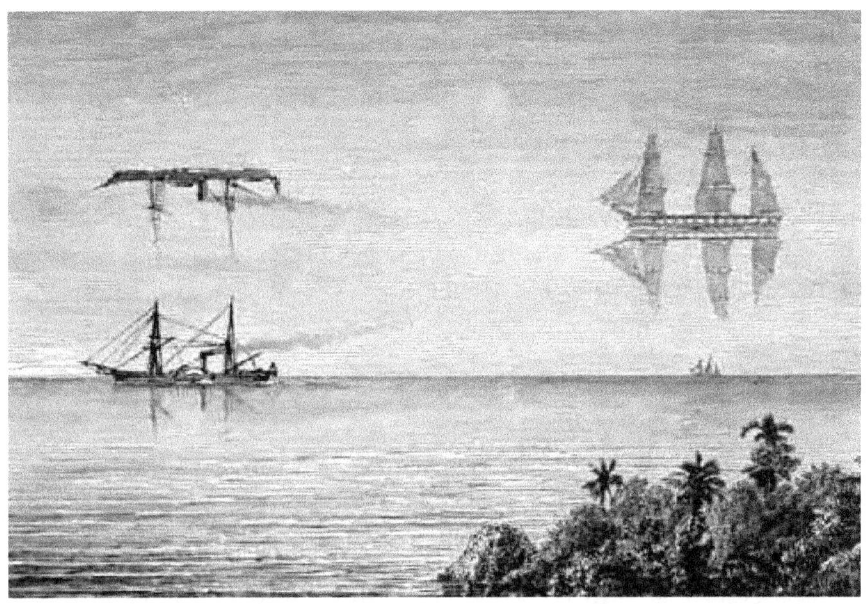

Non-uniform air temperatures cause the air to have uneven properties and cause light rays to bend -- not travel in straight lines. This illustration from an 1872 book by Frank Richard Stockton (1834-1902) shows the mirage phenomenon at sea, a form of refraction. Here a layer of warm air is above a layer of cold air, causing a quasi-reflection of the ship to appear in the sky. The 1665 Unidentified Flying Object (UFO) sighting over Stralsund, Germany could have been a mirage.

Mirages can also be seen on land, above the desert, or above a long, straight, hot highway. In these land cases, the warm layer of air is below the cold layer, and a quasi-reflection of the sky appears below on the hot surface. A parched desert traveler may think he sees a pool of water in the distance.

Refraction is often mentioned in conjunction with the difficulty of spear fishing. When viewed at a glancing angle, the fish in the water is not in the same straight-line direction as it appears to the spear fisher. See for yourself by holding a straight pencil partway into a bowl of water and experimenting with various pencil angles and viewing angles.

There are refraction phenomena seen elsewhere in nature in places like the rainbow. Inventions involving refraction are discussed in Part III, starting with the "Lenses" section.

The initial empirical understandings of refraction, where light does NOT travel in a straight line, developed through Ptolemy (100-170 CE), Alhazen (965-1040 CE), many others, and finally the waves of Maxwell's Equations.

Internet/Wikipedia search terms: mirage, rainbow, refraction, UFO 1665

Book references: Dampier 1948, Hecht 2017, Stockton 1872, Zajonc 1993

The 1872 CE drawing by Frank Richard Stockton (1834 – 1902) *Appearance in the air described as a mirage* is from p. 278 of the book *Round-about Rambles in Lands of Fact and Fancy* published by Scribner, Armstrong & Company in 1872. The photographic image of the drawing is taken from Wikipedia. Wikipedia states, "it is in the public domain in its country of origin and other countries and areas where the copyright term is the author's life plus 70 years or fewer."

Sunset

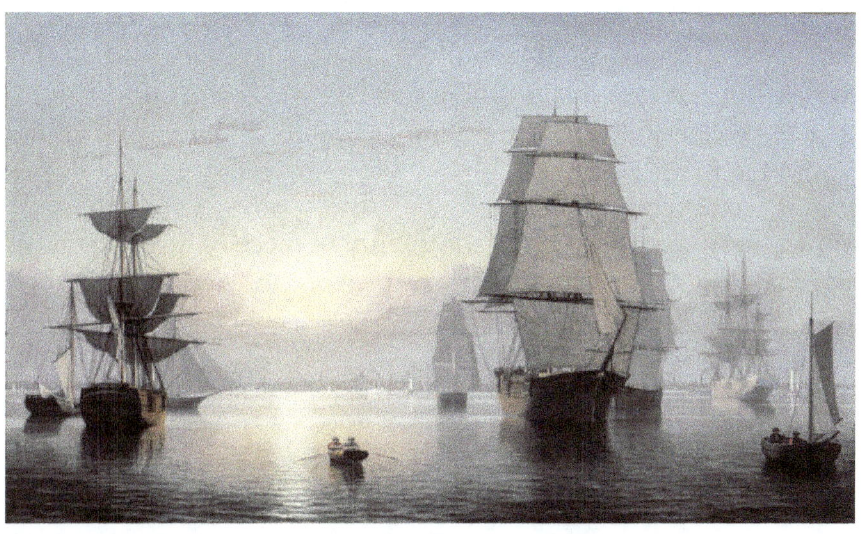

The painting *Boston Harbor, Sunset* by Fritz Henry Lane (1804-1865) shows several natural phenomena. The sunset features must have fascinated our ancestors since long before written history. These features took a long time for science to fully understand. The reflection of the Sun from the water surface was understood empirically by Euclid (born ~325 BCE), who viewed optics as subsidiary to geometry, and light as traveling in straight lines. The now largely complete scientific understanding of reflection required James Clerk Maxwell (1831-1879 CE) to first develop Maxwell's Equations. The shadows and reflections of the boats on the water are other examples of light traveling in straight lines.

The refraction of light in the atmosphere accounts for the apparently slow setting and occasional shape distortion of the Sun.

These are subtle Mirage phenomena as discussed in the previous section. Refer also to the "Refraction" section in Part I.

Why most of the sky remained blue, even at sunset, was a mystery until Lord Rayleigh (1842-1919 CE). He worked from 1871 to 1899 to come up with an accepted explanation, again with the help of Maxwell's Equations. The mechanism is now named for Rayleigh. He earned the 1904 Nobel Prize for discovering argon. Earlier, Newton (1624-1726 CE) understood that the white light from the Sun is actually a mixture of colors from blue to red.

Fortunately, appreciation of the beauty of these natural phenomena does not require an understanding of the science!

Internet/Wikipedia search terms: reflection, refraction, Rayleigh scattering, shadow, sunset

Book references: Hecht 2017

The circa 1850 CE painting *Boston Harbor, Sunset*, by artist Fritz Henry Lane (1804-1865) can be found at the Los Angeles County Museum of Art, Gift of Jo Ann and Julian Ganz, Jr., in honor of the museum's 25th anniversary, AC1993.229.1. The image shown here is in the public domain under LACMA's terms of use policy

Plants

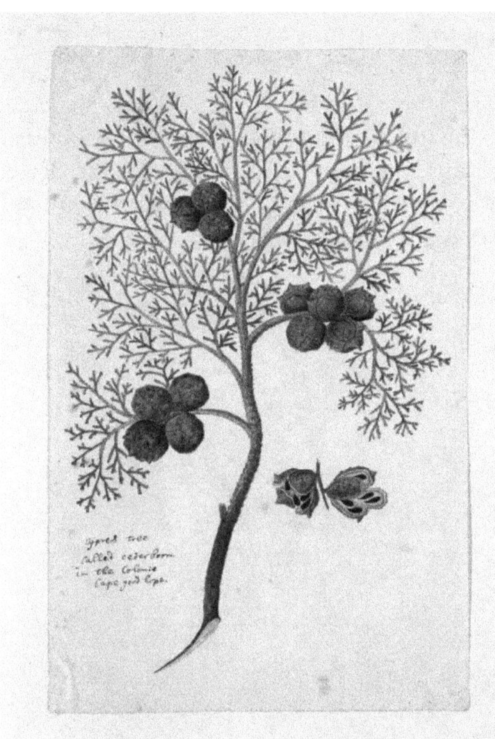

The drawing *Mountain cypress, or Cape cedar* by artist Robert Jacob Gordon (1743-1795) represents one of the two main branches of nature – plants. Plants started off in the ocean about a billion years ago, and had covered much of the land by about half a billion years ago. Many plants get their green color from the pigment chlorophyll, which is associated with photosynthesis.

Photosynthesis plays an extremely important role in life as it converts water and carbon dioxide to oxygen plus carbohydrates. While humans have known since the Neolithic Revolution that plants need water and sunlight, it wasn't until the 1950s that Melvin Calvin (1911-1997) and associates figured out that photosynthesis is a two-step process, part of which is now called the Calvin Cycle. The oxygen that plants release to the atmosphere comes from the water they take in. The energy in the carbohydrates comes from sunlight. Calvin received the Nobel Prize for this work in 1961.

Animal life, discussed soon in the "Animals" section, relies on photosynthesis – the oxygen for breathing, and the carbohydrates for food. The plants and animals have evolved to grow with the temperatures and light provided by the Sun.

Internet/Wikipedia search terms: plant, photosynthesis, Neolithic Revolution

Book references: Gross 2002, Russell 2017

The circa 1780 CE drawing *Widdringtonia nodiflora (L.) E. Powrie (Mountain cypress, or Cape cedar)* by artist Robert Jacob Gordon (1743-1795) can be found at the Rijksmuseum, The Gordon African Collection: Plants (RP-T-1914-18), Object Number: RP-T-1914-18-19. The image shown here is in the public domain under the Rijksmuseum's Creative Commons program.

Fire

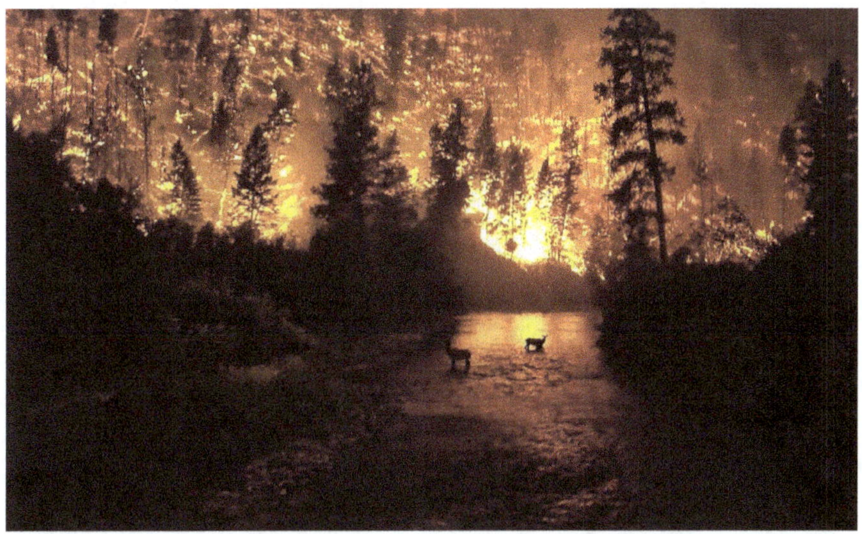

The photograph *Elk Bath – A wildfire in the Bitterroot National Forest in Montana*, taken by John McColgan, reminds us that fire occurred naturally long before our ancestors began learning to control it.

Fire requires three main ingredients – a source of fuel, oxygen, and a source of ignition. Ignition from early wildfires may have come from lightning, which was likely available long before the fuel and the oxygen.

While very primitive life may have begun in the oceans four billion years ago, the geological record suggests it took quite a while for photosynthesis to kick in. As stated earlier, plants started off in the ocean only one billion years ago, and then covered much of the land about half a billion years ago. By about 400 million years ago enough plant-generated oxygen had accumulated to support fire. Only then were all three ingredients in place – lightning for ignition, fuel, and oxygen. The latter two came from the plants. These early fires would have burned uncontrolled until self-extinguishing. For most of the last 400 million years there was an equilibrium between nature and fire.

Large wildfires give off lots of light, and are visible from outer space when looking at the dark side of the Earth.

Internet/Wikipedia search term: fire

Book reference: Pyne: 2019

The circa 2000 CE photograph *"Elk Bath" – A wildfire in the Bitterroot National Forest in Montana*, taken by John McColgan is found in Wikipedia. Wikipedia states, "this image or file is a work of a United States Department of Agriculture employee, taken or made as part of that person's official duties. As a work of the U.S. federal government, the image is in the public domain."

Animals

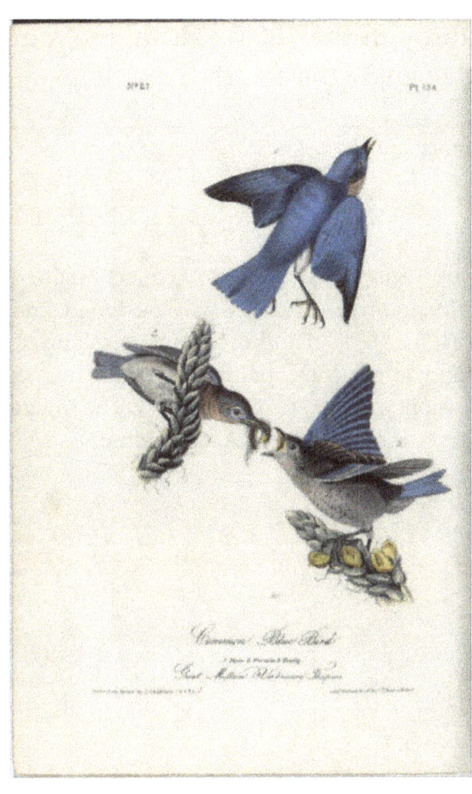

The colors and coloration found in nature are essential to the interrelationships between the many animals and plants, and must have been a source of aesthetic delight to our ancestors. These drawings of the *Common Bluebird*, also known as the Eastern Bluebird, were made circa 1840 CE by James Audubon (1785-1851).

Animals could not live without plants because they need the food and oxygen created by the plants via light and photosynthesis. The animals return the favor in a variety of ways, most notably helping plants to reproduce.

Returning to the bluebird, a couple of things are fascinating from the perspective of science and technology. First, because birds move so fast, it took a very long time for photography to become good enough to capture their live images – at least 150 years from the time of these Audubon drawings. The Peterson *Field Guide to the Birds* dated 2010 still contains artist drawings. Let's give credit to the quick eyes, memories, and skills of artists.

Second, the blue of the bluebird's feathers is created by the interference of light reflected from the structure of the feathers, a phenomenon understood only when light is viewed as waves. These "iridescence" effects are widespread in nature, primarily in animals. Other colors in nature are produced by pigments, better understood when light is viewed as particles. It took a while for science to sort this out, well through the 1800s. Meantime, our ancestors and artists continued to enjoy the color!

Internet/Wikipedia search terms: animals, animal coloration

Book reference: Russell 2017

The circa 1840 CE drawing of the *Common Blue Bird* is found in a collection titled *The Birds of America from Drawings Made in the United States* designed and published by John James Audubon (1785–1851). The lithographer is John T. Bowen (ca. 1801–?1856) It can be found at the Metropolitan Museum of Art, Bequest of Emma Sheafer, 1974, Accession Number 1974.661.4(1–7). The image shown here is in the public domain under the Met's Open Access initiative.

Pigmentation

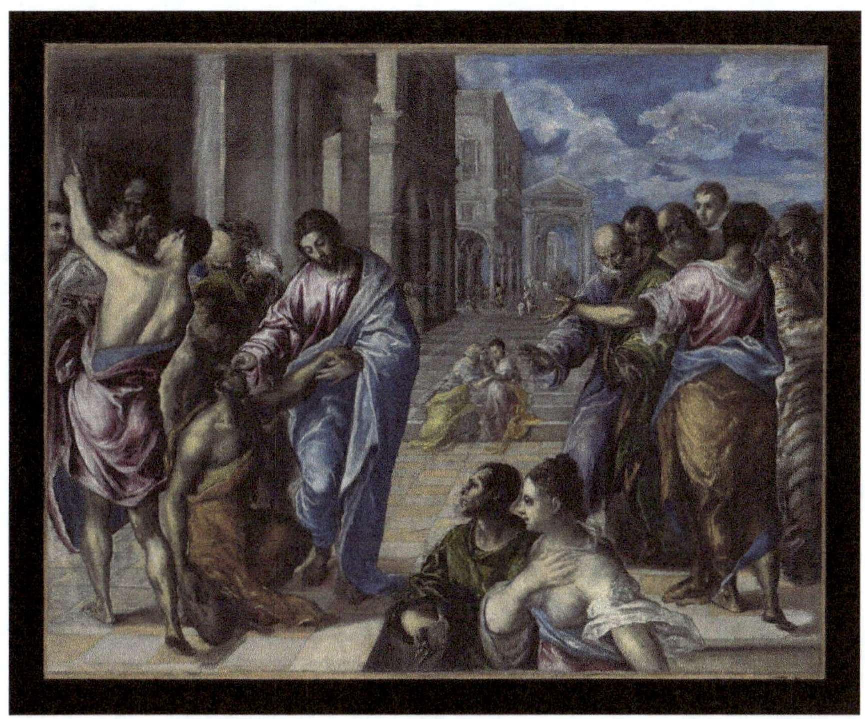

The 1570 painting *Christ Healing the Blind* by El Greco (1541-1614) shows a gathering of people representing a familiar Biblical story. A subtle feature in this painting is the variation in skin tones represented, something for which El Greco was known. In El Greco's Mediterranean world, variations in pigmentation were common as people from different cultures mingled.

Our human ancestors began migrating out of Equatorial Africa to populate the world starting roughly 50,000 years ago. The farther from the Equator they settled, the lighter their skin tones generally became over successive generations of genetic adaptation. Lighter skin is an advantage where there is less exposure to natural sunlight, because it helps the sunlight to penetrate and produce vitamin D. Vitamin D, in turn, helps prevent the deadly childhood disease of rickets. Darker skin is an advantage near the Equator because it helps prevent skin cancers.

The skin pigmentation story is more complicated than this, because of other factors such as diet and dress. One finds a variety of pigmentations among native people worldwide, and a great variety in places where global people mingle.

Apart from humans, there are few, if any, species that have successfully adapted to live year-round in our huge variety of global climates. More about this in the "Seasons and Poles" section of Part II.

Internet/Wikipedia search terms: human skin color, pigmentation, vitamin D

Book reference: Cavalli-Sforza 1995

The 1570 CE painting *Christ Healing the Blind* by El Greco (Domenikos Theotokopoulos) (1541–1614) can be found at the Metropolitan Museum of Art, Gift of Mr. and Mrs. Charles Wrightsman, 1978, Accession Number 1978.416. The image shown here is in the public domain under the Met's Open Access initiative.

Color Vision

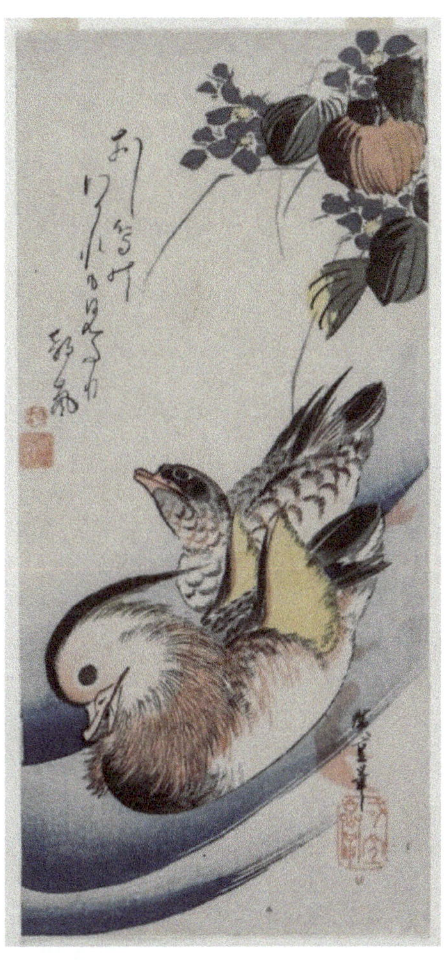

This colorful 1830s woodblock print by Japanese artist Utagawa Hiroshige (1797-1858) is titled *Mandarin Ducks and Flowering Plants*. It is just another example of the many unique colors displayed by plants and animals in nature. These colors play a critical role. Among animals, the colors allow species to identify one another, males to identify females, and vice-versa. Among plants, they allow specific species to attract specific animals as required for different reproductive purposes such as fertilization or spreading seeds. The colors change with geographic location. In many cases, the coloration of a specific species also changes with the seasons. The richness and diversity of this coloration is astonishing, and artists take full advantage.

Color vision relies on specialized receptors in the retina of the eye, and for each species the story is a little different. For humans, there are three receptors for task vision, designated S, M, and L, roughly sensitive to blue, green, and red respectively. In some humans the receptors respond differently, most commonly causing red-green color blindness. Vision systems of animal species vary widely — both in terms of color perception and in terms of visual acuity.

Internet/Wikipedia search terms: eye, color vision, color blindness, visual acuity

Book references: Gross 2002, Russell 2017

The circa 1830 CE color woodblock print Mandarin *Ducks and Flowering Plants* by Utagawa Hiroshige (1797–1858) can be found at the Cleveland Museum of Art, The Kelvin Smith Collection, given by Mrs. Kelvin Smith, Accession Number 1985.314. The image shown here is in the public domain under the CMA's Open Access initiative.

Sleep

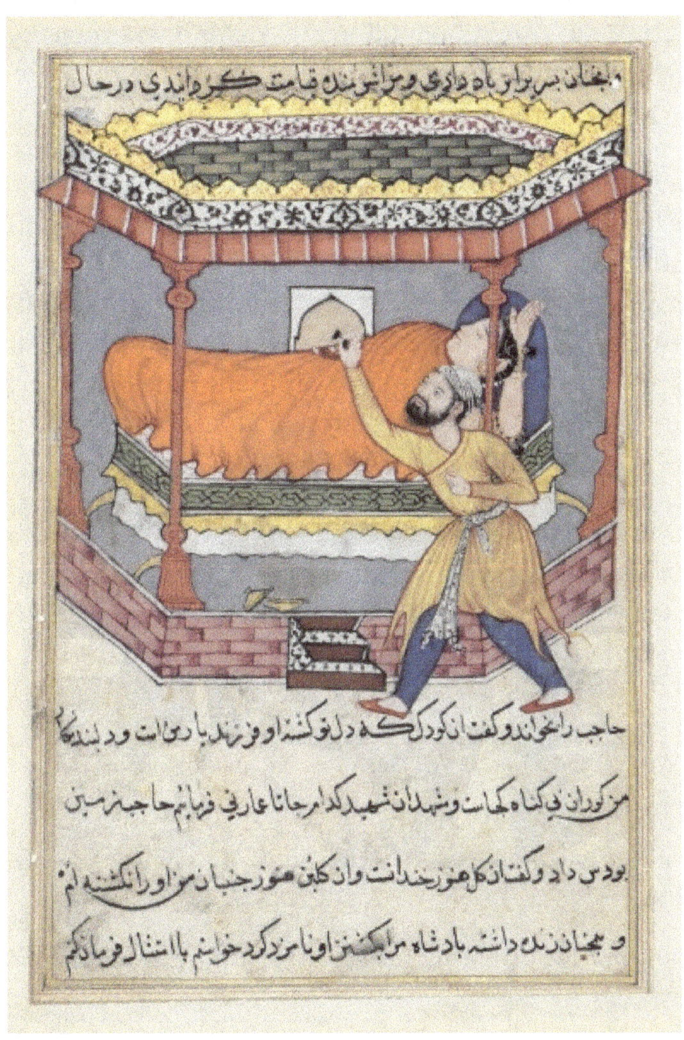

This art from India, 1560 CE, scripted *The king places the talisman on his sleeping wife,* reminds us of the importance of sleep to humans, and to other animals as well.

Sleep is an essential component of the 24-hour circadian rhythm controlled in nature by the rising and setting of the Sun. In humans, when the Sun goes down, the pituitary gland releases melatonin to the body, which induces sleep. The sleep proceeds through phases, and is essential to our health. When the Sun comes up, the melatonin release stops and our bodies wake up energized. They are maximally awake and energized around noon. It is primarily the blue in the light from the Sun which controls the melatonin release.

This can all go awry in modern times, when many of us are indoors, exposed to artificial sources of light at all hours of the day and night. Furthermore, during the day, most of us live indoors with lower light levels than would be found outdoors from the Sun. Our bodies may not be fully awake, even during the day. Careful attention to light levels at different times of day can help make us healthier and sleep better. This can also help us avoid Seasonal Affective Disorder (SAD).

There is a wide range of sleep cycles in nature. Nocturnal animals such as owls, bats, and some cats sleep during the day. Some bears hibernate, a very deep sleep, in the winter in cold climates. Each case is a little different, with each species adapted to its unique niche.

Internet/Wikipedia search terms: sleep, circadian rhythm, Seasonal Affective Disorder (SAD)

Book references: Gross 2002, Hansler 2022, Russell 2017, Walker 2017, Wetterberg 2017

The 1560 CE gum tempera, ink, and gold on paper *The king places the talisman on his sleeping wife*, from a Tuti-nama (*Tales of a Parrot*): Fiftieth Night by an unknown artist, Mughal India, court of Akbar, can be found at the Cleveland Museum of Art, Gift of Mrs. A. Dean Perry, Accession Number 1962.279.323.a. The image shown here is in the public domain under the CMA's Open Access initiative.

Seasons and Poles

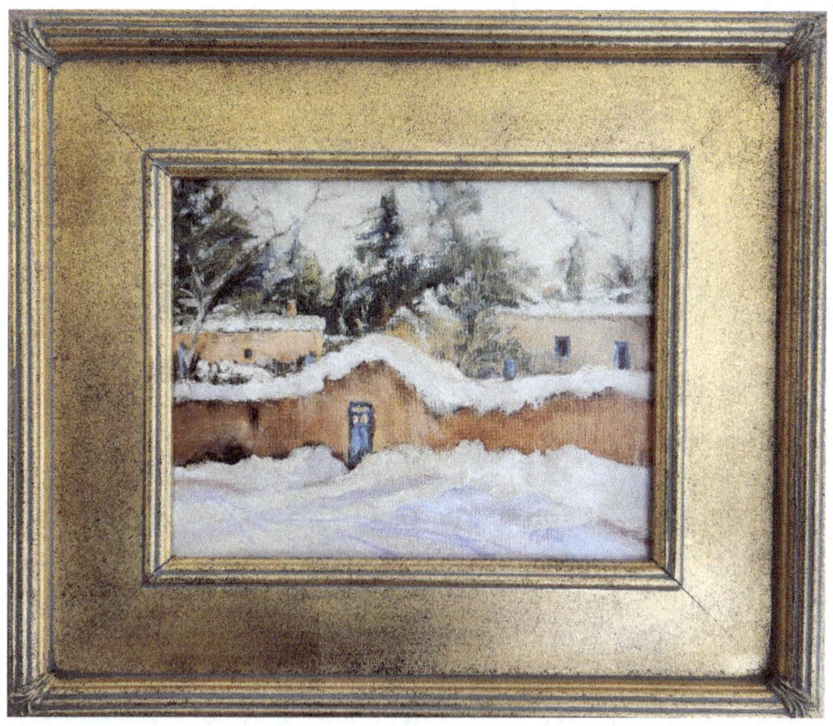

The painting *Taos Winter* by artist Cynthia Obermann (1940-) reminds us of the seasons, and of the increasingly cold temperatures and large winter-summer differences that occur moving away from the Equator. These result from the combination of the Earth's axis tilt relative to the Earth's orbit, and the increasingly oblique angle of the Sun's rays further from the Equator. At the poles there is no sunlight (with its accompanying heat) at all in the dead of winter. The winter cold is mitigated to some extent by the ocean currents, which bring warm water toward the poles, especially the North Pole. At the South Pole, the ocean currents do not help much due to the size of the Antarctic land mass.

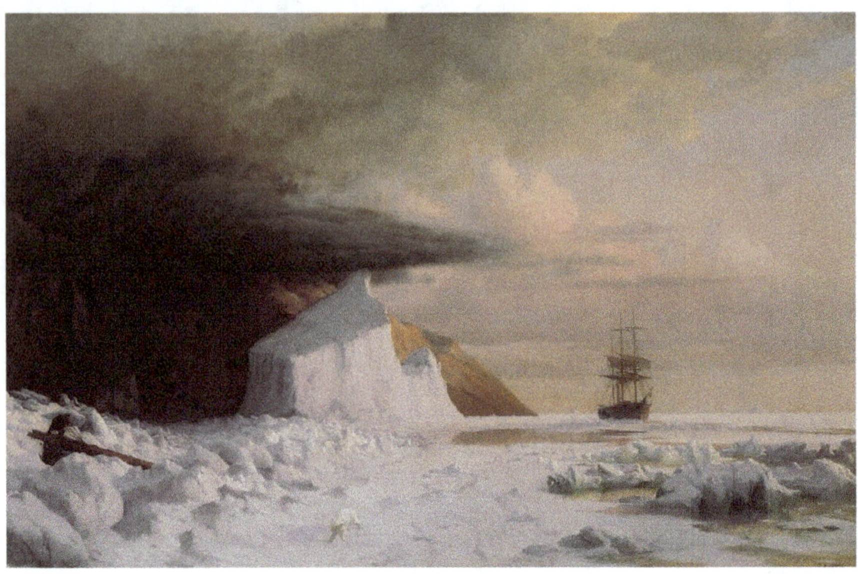

The 1871 painting *An Arctic Summer: Boring Through the Pack in Melville Bay* is by William Bradford (1823-1892). Melville Bay, off western Greenland, is north of the Arctic Circle, where the Sun never sets in the summer. The painting's inscription reads, "In 1861 the marine painter William Bradford made the first of his eight expeditions to the Arctic. This painting, based on photographs and sketches produced during his final trip, in 1869, shows the artist's steamer, Panther, plying its way through the summer ice along the northern coast of Greenland. Panther was one of numerous vessels engaged in the search for the Northwest Passage between the Atlantic and Pacific Oceans. According to Bradford's journal, the ship's crew had decided to hunt the polar bear seen in the foreground, 'anxious to possess so fine a skin,' but the bear made a parting glance over its shoulder before heading for the water, managing to escape its pursuers."

Over the past billion years, life has adapted to the climates and seasons in regions far from the Equator. In the harsher climates close to the poles, life is most dependent on the warmth provided by the ocean currents. The polar bear in the image, for instance, survives on the fish found in the waters. Few if any plants live here, even in summer. Climate history tells us that there have been periods when the Earth in general, and polar regions in particular, have been warmer and/or colder than recently.

Our human ancestors evolved to become homo sapiens close to the Equator in Africa about 300,000 years ago. They began migrating to colder climates closer to the poles about 50,000 years ago. The crossing from Eurasia to the Americas was facilitated by ice at the Bering Strait during the most recent ice age. By 10,000 years ago, all of the continents except Antarctica were populated.

The dramatic variations in light and temperature from season to season and from pole to equator to pole which underly this global migration and adaptation are the direct result of variations in light and heat from the Sun. The migrations of our ancestors were enabled and stimulated by the innate curiosity and adaptability of our homo sapiens species.

Internet/Wikipedia search terms: season, homo sapiens, evolution, climate history

Book references: Cavalli-Sforza 1995, Feder 2014, Russell 2017

The circa 2000 CE painting *Taos Winter* by Cynthia Obermann (1940-) is in the possession of the author, and its image is hereby placed in the public domain.

The 1871 CE painting *An Arctic Summer: Boring Through the Pack in Melville Bay* by William Bradford (1823–1892) can be found at the Metropolitan Museum of Art, Gift of Erving and Joyce Wolf, in memory of Diane R. Wolf, 1982, Accession Number 1982.443.1. The image shown here is in the public domain under the Met's Open Access initiative.

Bioluminescence

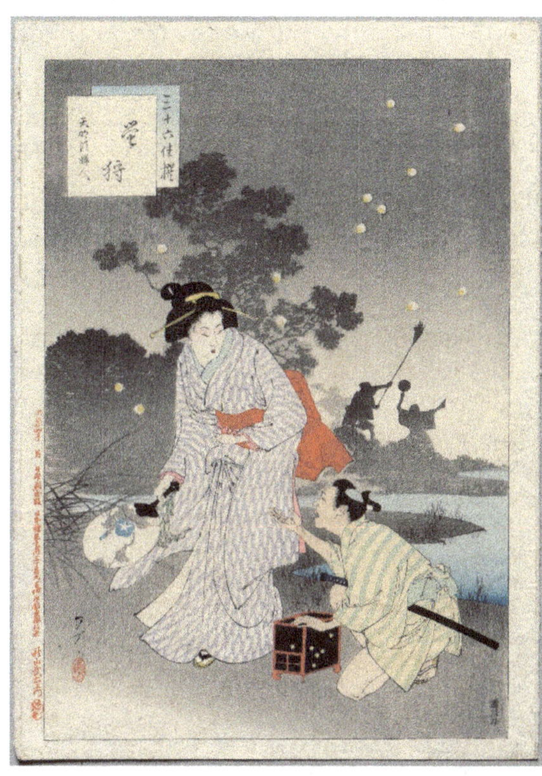

Much of the previous discussion has involved light associated with heat – from the Sun or from a fire. There is also a wide variety of light sources which are not hot, phenomena broadly categorized as cold light, also mentioned in the earlier discussion of aurora borealis. Another example is found in the painting *Chasing Fireflies, A Lady of the Tenmei Era (1781-1789)*, by Japanese artist Mizuno Toshikata (1866-1908). Fireflies are one example of bioluminescence.

Bioluminescence and other cold light phenomena were well known to our ancient ancestors and written about by Aristotle (384-322 BCE). Up until 200 years ago it was generally dark outside at night, due to the absence of modern electric lighting. People noticed and found pleasure in these phenomena. Sadly, today, bathed in nightly light pollution, people do not.

Cold light phenomena all involve mechanisms which in some way place atoms or molecules in unstable excited states. When these atoms or molecules decay to lower states, they emit photons of light. The unstable states are created, for instance, by a chemical reaction, or by absorption of a photon of light. While the terminology associated with these phenomena is confusing and inconsistent, the highest-level terms may be "cold" light or "luminescence". Harvey applies the term "luminescence" only to cold light.

Internet/Wikipedia search terms: cold light, bioluminescence, luminescence, phosphorescence

Book references: Dampier 1948, Gross 2002, Harvey 2005 Russell 2017

The 1894 CE woodblock print titled *Chasing Fireflies, A Lady of the Tenmei Era (1781-1789)*, from the series Thirty-six Elegant Selections by Mizuno Toshikata (1866–1908) can be found at the Cleveland Museum of Art, Gift of the Norman W. Zaworski Trust, Accession Number 2017.73. The image shown here is in the public domain under the CMA's Open Access initiative.

PART III

HUMAN INVENTION

Genesis 1

26 And God said, Let us make man in our image, after our likeness: and let them have dominion over the fish of the sea, and over the fowl of the air, and over the cattle, and over all the earth, and over every creeping thing that creepeth upon the earth.

King James Bible

The natural phenomena in Part II are all things with which modern humans are familiar. The examples and artwork are all from relatively modern times. Yet, the phenomena were all out there in nature long before our brains got bigger and our ancestors became homo sapiens roughly 300,000 years ago. Our most ancient ancestors would have noticed them.

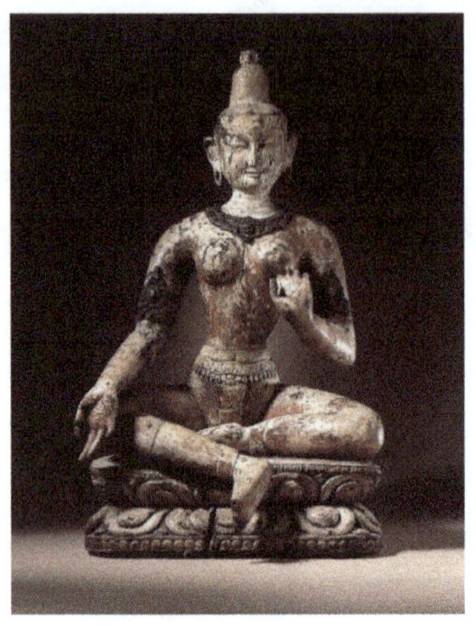

The Nepalese wood sculpture titled *The Buddhist Goddess Victorious Wisdom Tara* reminds us that once homo sapiens had acquired our larger brains, they increased in intelligence. They became wiser. They started using those brains, and the wisdom that went with them, to invent things. Perhaps they started with stone tools, at least 400,000 years ago. Some argue that the stone tools in museums are sometimes nicer than they needed to be, and therefore represent extremely early art. I defer to the reader and experts on this point, and only refer to the later cave paintings as early art.

I will next turn to the many human inventions involving light which result from our larger brains and wisdom. The rough sequence of invention is as follows:

~ 1 million years ago – controlled fire, stone tools,

~ 20,000 years ago – oil lamps, cave painting,

~ 12,000 years ago – Neolithic agriculture begins, settlements, religion, written language

~ 2,000-3,000 years ago – candles, early philosophy/science, burning glass, mirror, camera obscura, increased trade,

~ 1,000 years ago – better lenses enabling telescopes, microscopes, eyeglasses,

~ 200 years ago – photography,

~ 100 years ago – electric lighting, and

~ 50 years ago – television, photonics.

Internet/Wikipedia search terms: brain, homo sapiens, intelligence, invention

Book references: Feder 2014, Watson 2006

The circa 15th century CE sculpture in wood with traces of paint having copper ornaments inlaid with gemstones titled *The Buddhist Goddess Victorious Wisdom Tara (Jina-Prajna Tara)*, Nepal, can be found at the Los Angeles County Museum of Art, From the Nasli and Alice Heeramaneck Collection, Museum Associates Purchase, M.72.1.10. The image shown here is in the public domain under LACMA's terms of use policy.

Controlled Fire

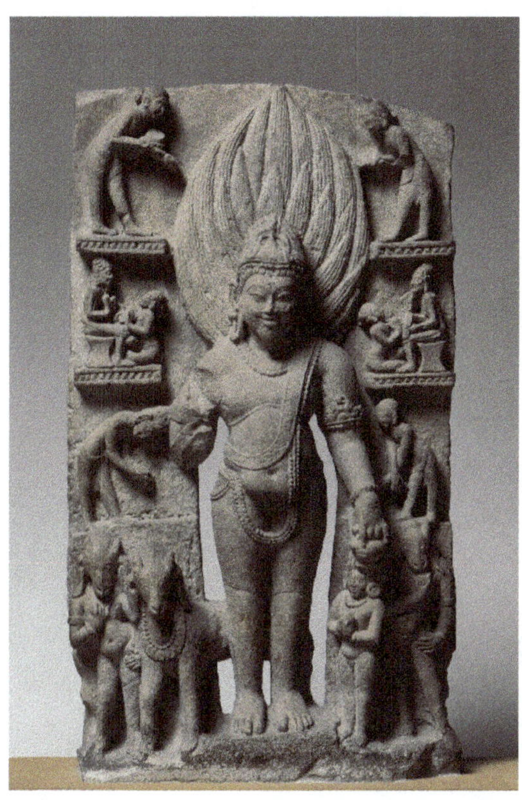

Controlled fire is very important in much of Part III. Controlled fire plays a large role in early mythology and religion. This sandstone carving from India circa 1000 CE is titled *Agni, God of Fire*. In Hindu cosmology Agni and fire represent just one of five pairs of gods and elements. The five Hindu elements are earth, air, fire, sky, and water.

Recall from the Introduction to Part I that in the Greek philosophy of Empedocles (circa 494 – 434 BCE) fire is one of the four elements – earth, air, fire, and water. Also, in Greek mythology, Prometheus is said to have stolen fire from the gods, and then been severely punished.

An extensive list of gods representing fire in indigenous mythologies worldwide can be found in Wikipedia.

Going much further back in time than these fire gods, one of our ancestors' first inventions is thought to have been stone tools. In the same uncertain time frame, about a million years ago, long before they became homo sapiens with our now larger brains, and long before they developed their fire gods, they learned to control fire. This all took place in Africa. This allowed our ancestors to cook and to stay warm at night with a little light.

Imagine how the early control of fire might have come about. Perhaps our ancestor, at the edge of a natural forest fire, saw some benefit, and put some sticks on it to keep it going, or learned to move it. Then, there was the challenge of starting (igniting) a new one, perhaps by rubbing sticks together.

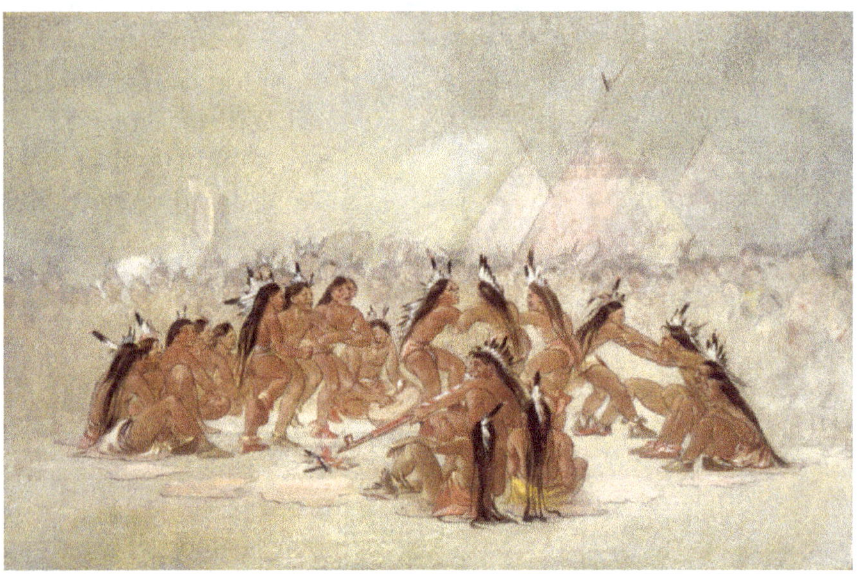

Above, the 1835 CE painting titled *Pipe Dance, Assiniboine* is by George Catlin (1796-1872). It shows controlled fire at the center of a Native American dance ceremony in what is now south-central Canada. The museum caption reads in part, "In the centre and by the fire, was seated a dignitary, who seemed to be a chief . . . another grim-visaged fellow in another part of the group, commenced beating on a drum or tambourine, accompanied by his voice; when one of the young men seated, sprang instantly on his feet, and commenced singing in time with the taps of the drum, and leaping about on one foot and the other in the most violent manner imaginable…" This was just about 200 years ago, pretty recent on the million-year time scale of controlled fire.

Controlled fire has been important throughout human history as a source of light, heat, and of other things as well. The primitive torch may be viewed as an extension of controlled fire – just take a burning stick out by its cold end and you have a torch. Controlled fire would have been increasingly important in the migration away from the equator discussed in the "Seasons and Poles" section of Part II. The colder the climate, the more important the fire to keep warm. Controlled fire came well before anything known of early religion, as in the fire gods mentioned above, and as discussed in the "Religion" section later in Part III. Few if any of the inventions that follow in Part III would have occurred without controlled fire coming first.

Controlled fire still plays a central role in our modern culture today. Environmentalists would like to reduce our reliance on fire for cooking, heating, producing electricity, etc. so as to reduce the emission of carbon dioxide, a greenhouse gas which contributes to climate change.

Internet/Wikipedia search terms: fire, Prometheus, Agni, climate change

Book references: Dampier 1948, Feder 2014, Pyne 2019

The circa 1000 CE sandstone titled *Agni, God of Fire*, from India can be found at the Cleveland Museum of Art, Edward L. Whittemore Fund, Accession Number 1955.51. The image shown here is in the public domain under the CMA's Open Access initiative.

The 1835-1837 CE painting *Pipe Dance, Assiniboine* by George Catlin (1796 –1872) can be found at the Smithsonian American Art Museum, Gift of Mrs. Joseph Harrison, Jr., Accession Number 1985.66.453. The Smithsonian American Art Museum identifies this image as free to use.

Oil Lamps

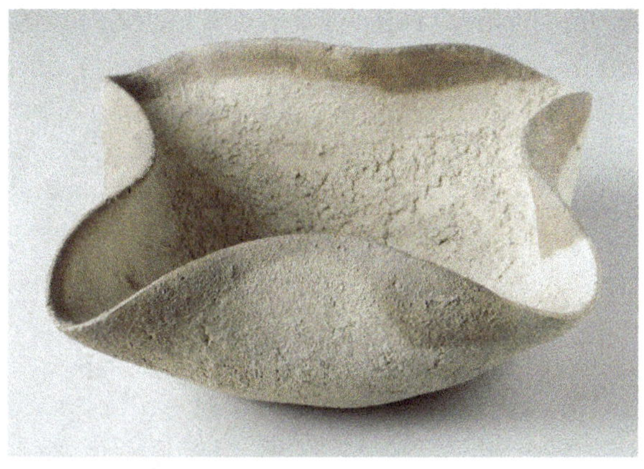

This *Four-Wick Oil Lamp* from Israel is made of ceramic and dated circa 2000 BCE. Each corner accommodates one wick, which dips into the oil and feeds a flame at its outer end. Oil lamps were an early application of controlled fire as a low-smoke indoor light source. Ones not unlike this are still in use today for ceremonial purposes, as well as for generating light in places without electricity. Olives had been domesticated by the time of this lamp, and olive oil may have been its fuel.

The earliest known oil lamps were more primitive, did not have wicks, and more likely used animal fat as a fuel. Something simpler such as a hollowed-out stone or a sea shell would work. A beautiful one found in the Lascaux caves is carved from red sandstone and dates to around 15,000 BCE. This would have been *before* the Neolithic Revolution, when our ancestors had populated the earth and begun to live in settled communities with agriculture.

Oil lamps have evolved considerably in the past 4,000 years to accommodate more sophisticated wick mechanisms, glass chimneys to shield the flame from wind, metallic structures to hold the fuel and support the parts, mirrors to direct the light, and a variety of fuels ranging from whale oil to kerosene. The modern versions of oil lamps were the dominant source of indoor lighting until electric lighting came along. However, even by the 1920s, in the US, electricity had reached only about a third of the homes. At that time, electric lighting, and the gas lighting which preceded it by a few decades, only reached urban areas with high population densities. Even today, oil lamps are a viable source of indoor lighting for people living off the electrical grid. Candles, to be discussed later in the "Candles" section, are more expensive to use.

Internet/Wikipedia search terms: indoor lighting, Lascaux, kerosene lamp, oil lamp, wick

Book references: Bailey 1963, DiLaura 2006, O'Dea 1958

The circa 2000 BCE *Four-Wick Oil Lamp* from Israel can be found at the Los Angeles County Museum of Art, Anonymous gift (M.91.364.8). The image shown here is in the public domain under LACMA's terms of use policy.

Agriculture

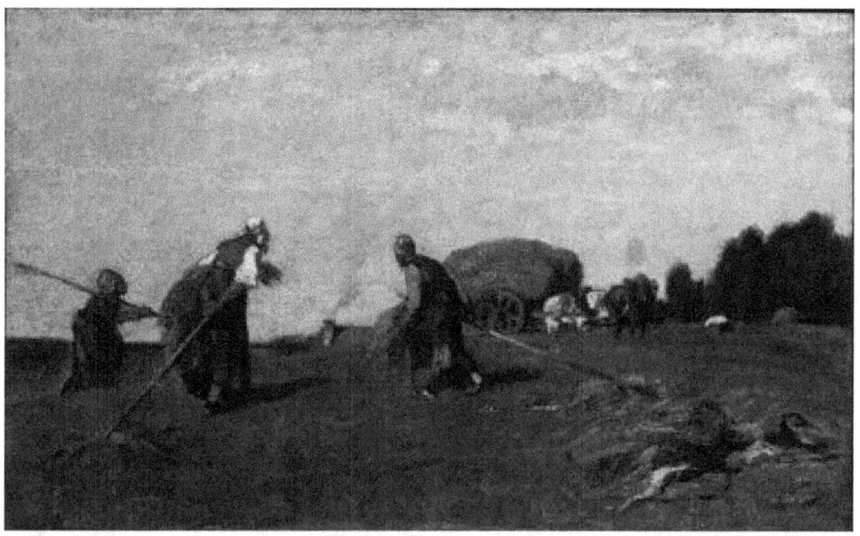

By roughly 10,000 years ago, after the last ice age, our human ancestors had spread world-wide, and then gradually stopped being hunter-gatherers. In harsher climates, far from the Equator especially, this required that they remain at one location so as to store crops for the winter which they had grown during summer. Both plants and animals were domesticated to suit the local climate and lifestyle. The 1851 CE painting by Eugène Fromentin (1820-1876) titled *The Reapers* reflects a settled agricultural lifestyle which had not changed much for 10,000 years. The painting's museum description says, "Fromentin depicts the close of the working day as colorfully garbed peasants drag their implements toward an oxcart heavily laden with their harvest. Smoke curls from a chimney in the distance, suggesting the additional reward of a warm hearth."

Deciding where to settle required careful consideration. Water and light were required for the plants to grow. Plants had to be chosen that could grow and produce in the local location and climate. Also, especially important moving away from the Equator was knowing when to plant. This required keeping track of the seasons with structures such as Stonehenge to track the Sun.

Our ancestors' advance, from moving around as hunter-gatherers to settling in communities with agriculture, is referred to as the Neolithic Revolution. Archeology tells us that this began about 12,000 years ago in the Fertile Crescent, defined by the Tigris and Euphrates rivers. Over the next several thousand years it had occurred worldwide in varying degrees and different ways, lastly in the Americas.

Internet/Wikipedia search terms: agriculture, civilization, Neolithic Revolution, Stonehenge

Book reference: Feder 2014

The 1851 CE painting *The Reapers* by Eugène Fromentin (1820-1876) can be found at the Brooklyn Museum, Bequest of William H. Herriman, Accession Number 21.124. The Brooklyn Museum states there are no known copyright restrictions.

Windows

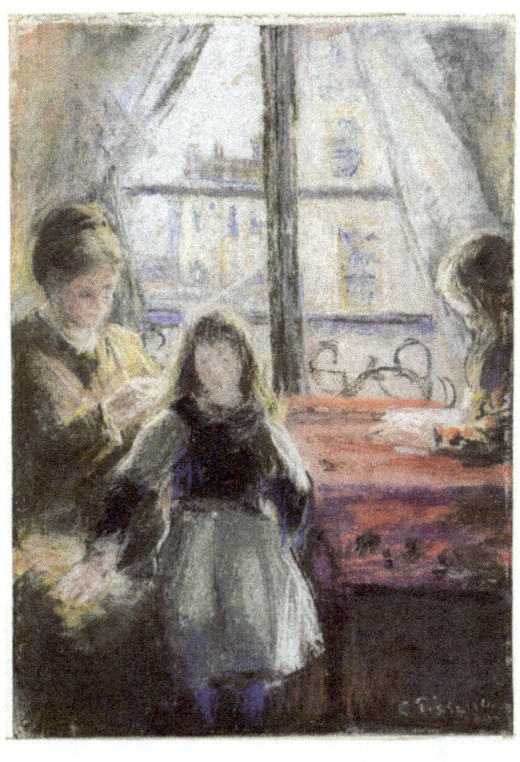

Around the same time that groups of our ancestors began settling in specific places so as to domesticate animals and cultivate crops, they also began to construct permanent buildings in their settlements. This was after the last ice age, more recent than 10,000 years ago. The buildings soon had windows to let in the light and to see out, much the same function as the window in this 1878 CE pastel *At the Window* by French artist Camille Pissarro (1830-1903). The museum description states that "Even indoors, Pissarro found a way to investigate the effects of natural light, which is characteristic of his Impressionist style."

The earliest windows would not have had glass, which did not come along until the Roman era, perhaps 2,000 years ago. Glass would only have been for the wealthy. Before glass, something so simple as an animal hide might have been used to exclude foul weather.

Modern glass windows have double glazing for thermal

insulation, sophisticated mechanisms for opening and closing, screens for excluding insects, and some form of shades for blocking light when needed.

To this day, however, even in a modern house with modern electric lighting, the best light for performing a task requiring good eyesight and bright light can often be found at a window. Many artists prefer to work near large windows having northern exposure (in the northern hemisphere) so as to provide uniform, full spectrum white light without the glare of direct sunlight.

Internet/Wikipedia search term: window

Book references: Feder 2014

The 1878 CE pastel titled *At the Window, rue des Trois Frères* by artist Camille Pissarro (1830–1903) can be found at the Art Institute of Chicago, Gift of Dorothy Braude Edinburg to the Harry B. and Bessie K. Braude Memorial Collection, Reference Number 2012.89. The image shown here is in the public domain under the museum's Creative Commons program.

Religion

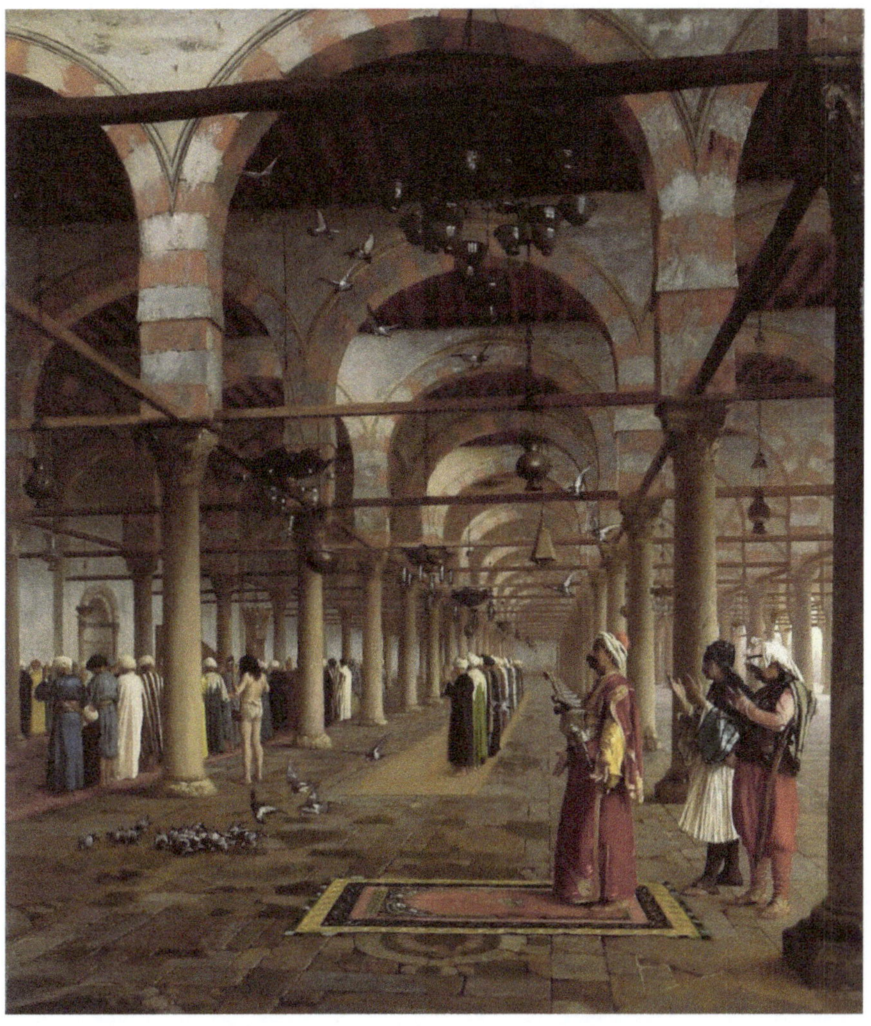

The 1871 painting *Prayer in the Mosque* by Jean-Léon Gérôme (1824-1904) depicts the interior of the seventh-century mosque of 'Amr in Cairo. It was painted after the artist's visit to Egypt in

1868. Judaism, Christianity, and Islam, the three Abrahamic religions, have played a major role in world religion for about two millennia. They all respect the creation story found in the book of Genesis, where God creates light in Chapter 1, Verse 3. Many modern adherents find meaning in the Genesis account even without literal, scientific acceptance.

Stepping back from specific religions, Barbara Sproul argues that creation myths "deal with first causes, the essences of what their cultures perceive reality to be. In them people set forth their primary understandings of man and world, time and space. And in them cultures express most directly, before they become involved in the fine points of sophisticated dogma, their understanding of awe before the absolute reality, the most basic fact of being." [Sproul 1979, p. 7] The same basic need for *primary understandings* exists today, although many find their answers outside of traditional religions.

Taking religion to flow from an innate human need for *primary understandings*, its origins go back further in time than there are any explicit records. What archeologists know of the origins of organized religion dates back to around 10,000 years ago. This was about the time, after the last ice age, during the Neolithic Revolution, that our ancestors were settling down to form civilizations around the world. They were beginning the cultivation of crops, and the building of what were to become cities.

This archeological dating places early religion well before the literal Genesis story. Scholars who have tried to count back through the Bible stories date the Genesis story to only around 6,000 years ago. This likely predated written language sophisticated enough for the written Genesis.

It is, thus, not surprising that creation stories from different isolated civilizations around the world should come down to us first through word of mouth, and, eventually, through writing, somewhat different from one another.

What is remarkable is the extent to which Sproul finds common themes in creation myths from isolated cultures around the world. One such theme is the creation of order out of chaos, an example of which is separating light from darkness. The Sun, and other celestial objects, play a prominent role in many creation myths and early religions. The Sun sometimes appears as sacred, a god or goddess. Our ancestors, whoever they were, felt that something special was going on with light and the Sun. This is not surprising because the Sun and its sunlight were so essential to their agriculture and survival. A modern cosmologist, who may feel that science holds many of the answers, likely agrees with the importance of light, as manifests in the Big Bang, expanding universe, and much of modern science.

The fire gods discussed earlier in the "Controlled Fire" section of Part II do not appear as involved in creation myths as do the Sun and the separation of light from darkness. The fire gods must, however, be viewed as part of early religion, and likely part of many non-Abrahamic religions today. There is so much that is not known about the origins and interconnections of early religions because it all happened long before written language.

Internet/Wikipedia search terms: religion, creation

Book references: Armstrong 2005, Campion 2012, Feder 2014, Polkinghorne 1989, Sproul 1979, Tyson 2017

The 1871 painting *Prayer in the Mosque* by Jean-Léon Gérôme (1824–1904) can be found at the Metropolitan Museum of Art, Catharine Lorillard Wolfe Collection, Bequest of Catharine Lorillard Wolfe, 1887, Accession Number 87.15.130. The image shown here is in the public domain under the Met's Open Access initiative

Written Language

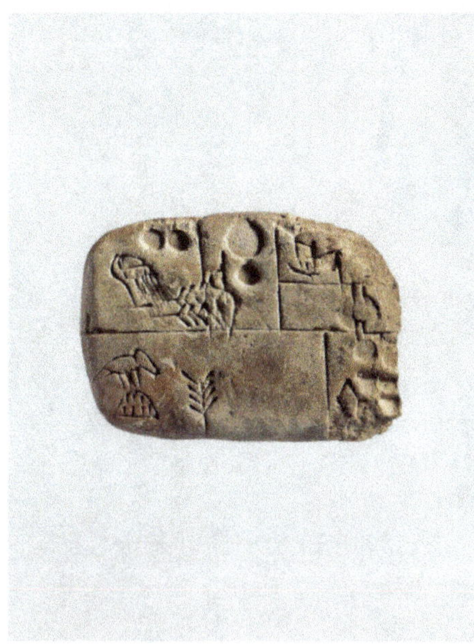

Archeologists say that simple written language, another human invention, dates back to as much as 9,000 years ago. This, again, was around the time that agriculture, permanent buildings, and religion began appearing. Like agriculture, writing may have occurred first around the Fertile Crescent, to serve an essential role in record keeping. The clay Sumerian cuneiform tablet labeled *administrative account concerning the distribution of barley and emmer*, dated 3100–2900 BCE, is a utilitarian example of art.

Written language relies heavily on light, our eyes, and vision, our ability to see symbols with our eyes, and thereby both store and retrieve information outside of our brains.

While 9,000-year-old agriculture and buildings would still be recognized and function as such today, written language has evolved enormously around the world to encompass a wide variety of functions, symbol systems, and languages.

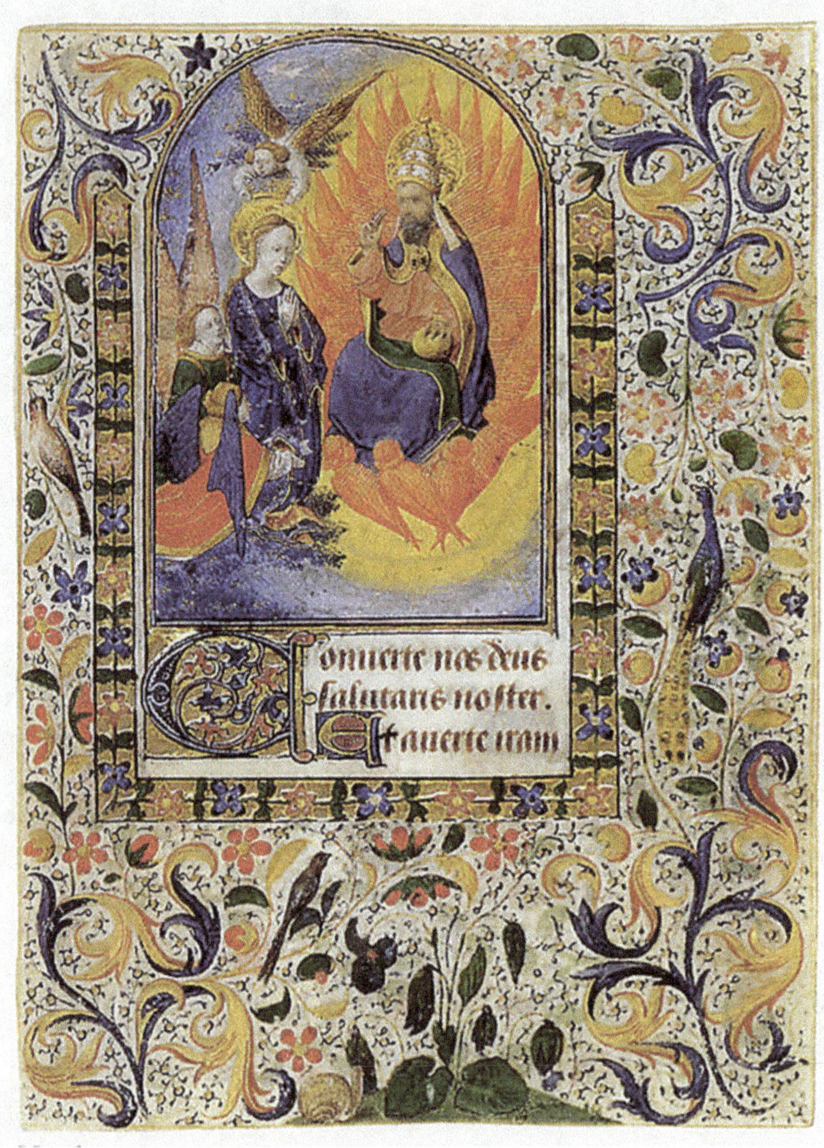

The 1455-60 CE tempera and gold leaf on parchment illustration titled *Coronation of the Virgin* shows one example of the extent to which written language has evolved over the millennia. Its museum description reads, "The book of hours to which this beautiful illumination belonged must have been a deluxe work commissioned by a wealthy patron. Both sides of the leaf are decorated with elaborate floral borders, and all the pages of the original manuscript probably were illuminated. This 'Coronation of the Virgin' depends on a composition by the Limbourg brothers, the Franco-Netherlandish illuminators responsible for the 'Belles Heures' of Jean de Berry. This leaf, however, was illuminated several decades later, probably in Paris."

The boundary between written language and art is indeed blurred in this example!

Written language up through these examples relied on individual craftsmanship, skill, and even sometimes artistry. This changed when Johannes Gutenberg (c. 1393/1406-1468 CE) invented movable type and the printing press. The printing press also enabled mass production of some forms of art. Written documents could be mass produced. Individual documents, however, remained largely hand-written or eventually type-written until the computer came along.

Internet/Wikipedia search terms: written language, printing press

Book reference: Feder 2014

The 3100–2900 BCE clay cuneiform tablet labeled *administrative account concerning the distribution of barley and emmer* (Sumerian) can be found at the Metropolitan Museum of Art, Purchase, Raymond and Beverly Sackler Gift, 1988, Accession Number 1988.433.2. The image shown here is in the public domain under the Met's Open Access initiative.

The 1455–60 CE book illustration labeled *Coronation of the Virgin* dates to and is attributed to an unknown French artist likely based in Paris. It can be found at the Metropolitan Museum of Art, Robert Lehman Collection, 1975, Accession Number 1975.1.2480. The image shown here is in the public domain under the Met's Open Access initiative.

Art

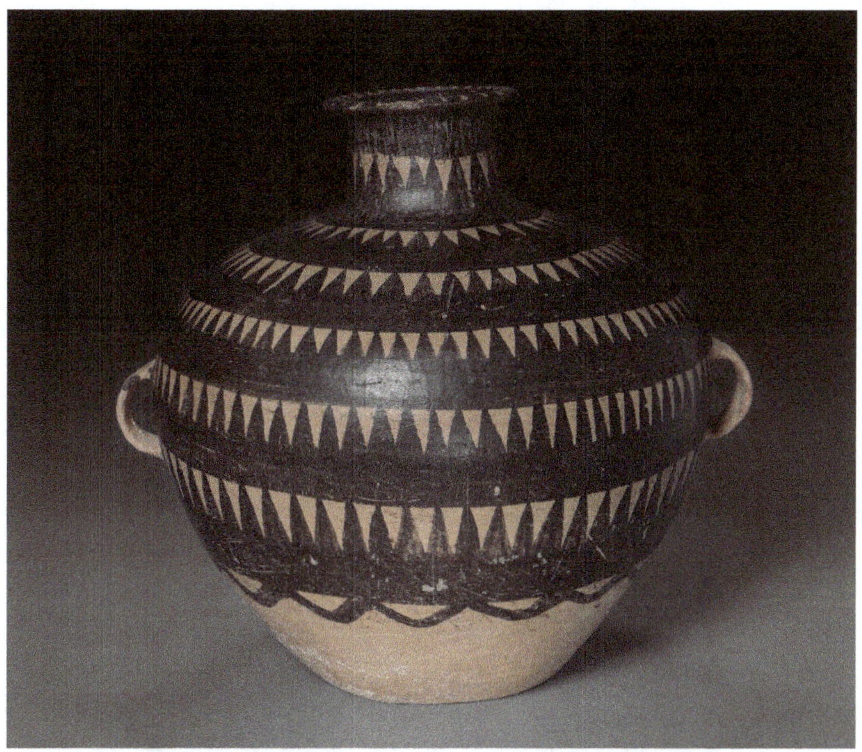

The earthenware with slip-painted decoration *Urn with Triangular Patterns* c. 3300–c. 2000 BCE is from Northwest China, Neolithic period, Majiayao culture. It serves as a reminder that art and artists have been around for a very long time, and throughout the world.

The word *art* as defined by Merriam-Webster has several somewhat different meanings. The one I use here is "the conscious use of skill and creative imagination especially in the production of aesthetic objects." Something utilitarian is not necessarily art, but can be art if it has an aesthetic aspect, as in the 4,000 to 5,000-year-old earthenware example. Our discussion here is narrowed to visual art, which inherently involves light – art that can be seen. Some of the other images found in the "Human Inventions" Part III of this book qualify as art even though they may also be of utilitarian objects.

This similarly utilitarian 900-1100 CE hammered gold *Beaker with Shells* from the Lambayeque (Sicán) people, Central Andes, surely also qualifies as art. (A gold object like this makes it obvious why the Spanish took such a predatory interest in the Americas a few centuries later.)

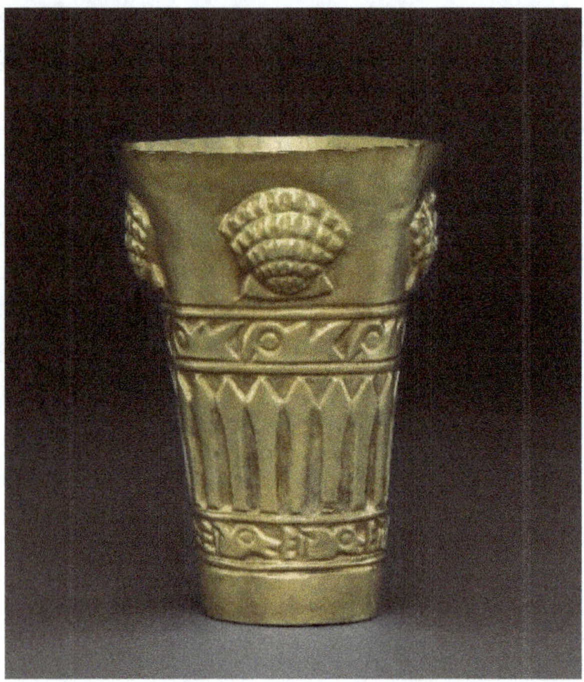

The 2,000-year-old terracotta head shown next is another, but less utilitarian, example of art, this one from West African Nok culture. The museum listing states, "This complete head's bold modeling, deliberate asymmetry, and sensitive expression make it one of the finest known examples of Nok sculpture."

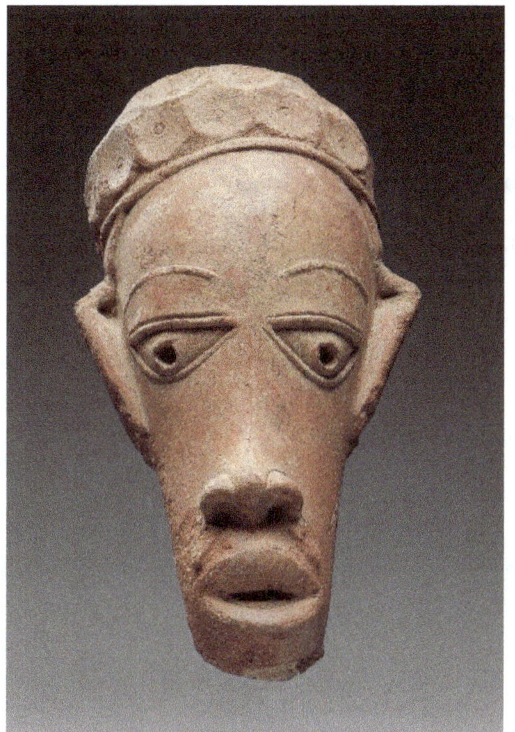

The earthenware urn, gold cup, and terracotta head exhibit totally different artistic skills, are from three different continents, and were crafted a few thousand years apart from one another. They are from early cultures. They are all pleasing to the eye, even today, thereby part of the story of art, human invention, and light. Interest in artistic beauty is innately human and worldwide.

One wonders how much early art has been lost for lack of modern museums and preservation means.

Art has been around for a very long time. How long can be debated. The cave paintings found at Lascaux, France, and elsewhere date back 15,000 to 30,000 years, depending on which cave. These are definitely art as they involve images with color. Archeologists have found even earlier examples and evidence of what some would call art.

Internet/Wikipedia search terms: art, visual arts

Book references: Clair 2017, Feder 2014, Janson 1986, Zuffi 2012

The 3300–2000 BCE earthenware with slip-painted decoration *Urn with Triangular Patterns* is from Northwest China, Neolithic period, Majiayao culture. It can be found at the Cleveland Museum of Art, Gift of Donna and James Reid, Accession Number 2017.21. The image shown here is in the public domain under the CMA's Open Access initiative.

The 900-1100 CE *Beaker with Shells* is from the Central Andes (Peru), Lambayeque (Sicán) people. It can be found at the Cleveland Museum of Art, Severance and Greta Millikin Purchase Fund, Accession Number 2015.8. The image shown here is in the public domain under the CMA's Open Access initiative.

The 20-620 CE terracotta *Head* is from the West Africa, Nigeria, Nok-culture style region, unknown maker. It can be found at the Cleveland Museum of Art, Andrew R. and Martha Holden Jennings Fund, Accession Number 1995.21. The image shown here is in the public domain under the CMA's Open Access initiative.

Pigments

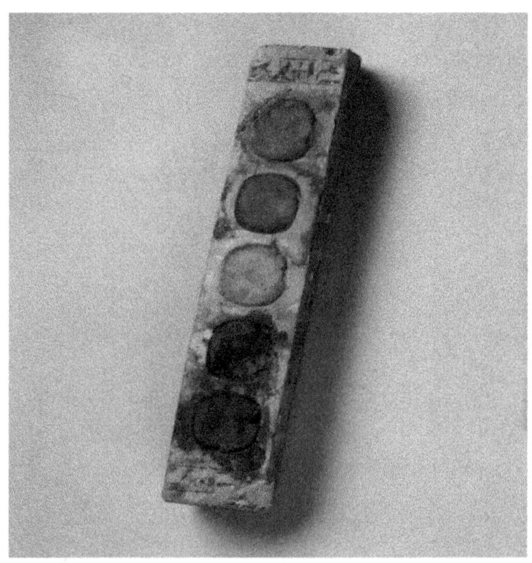

The object *Paint Box of Vizier Amenemope* (1425–1400 BCE) reminds us that art with color, be it painting, ceramics, or textiles, usually requires pigments to provide the color. This paintbox, from roughly 4,000 years ago in Egypt, tells us that the pigment industry has been alive for quite a while. The object's museum description says, "This paint box still preserves its original cakes of pigment: one cake each of red (red ocher), blue (Egyptian blue), green (a mixture of Egyptian blue, yellow ocher, and orpiment) and two of black (carbon black, from charcoal). It belonged to Amenemope, who was vizier, or prime minister, under Amenhotep II. Amenemope probably used his paint box for recreation."

Pigments have a fascinating history. The ochers come from iron-rich rocks which can be found around the world, and can be processed to provide a variety of colors. The blacks come from charcoal, which can be taken from fire remains.

An interesting story is the deep blue ultramarine, which is derived from the mineral lapis lazuli, a semi-precious stone. This mineral was discovered and mined in Afghanistan thousands of years ago, and traded via the Silk Road. This made it so expensive that into the Middle Ages some artists could not afford it. Another interesting story is Scheele's Green, which was developed by Swedish chemist Carl Wilhelm Scheele in 1775. Scheele's green became wildly popular throughout Europe, used in fabrics, wall papers, and even food coloring. Because it was arsenic-based, it led to widespread arsenic poisoning and likely some deaths.

Over the past century pigments have become increasingly synthetic, stable, and non-toxic.

Internet/Wikipedia search terms: art, lapis lazuli, pigment, ochre or ocher, paint, Scheele's Green

Book references: Clair 2017, Zuffi 2012

The 1425–1400 BCE object *Paint Box of Vizier Amenemope*, Egypt, New Kingdom (1540–1069 BCE), Dynasty 18, reign of Amenhotep II, can be found at the Cleveland Museum of Art, Gift of the John Huntington Art and Polytechnic Trust, Accession Number 1914.680. The image shown here is in the public domain under the CMA's Open Access initiative.

Optical Illusions

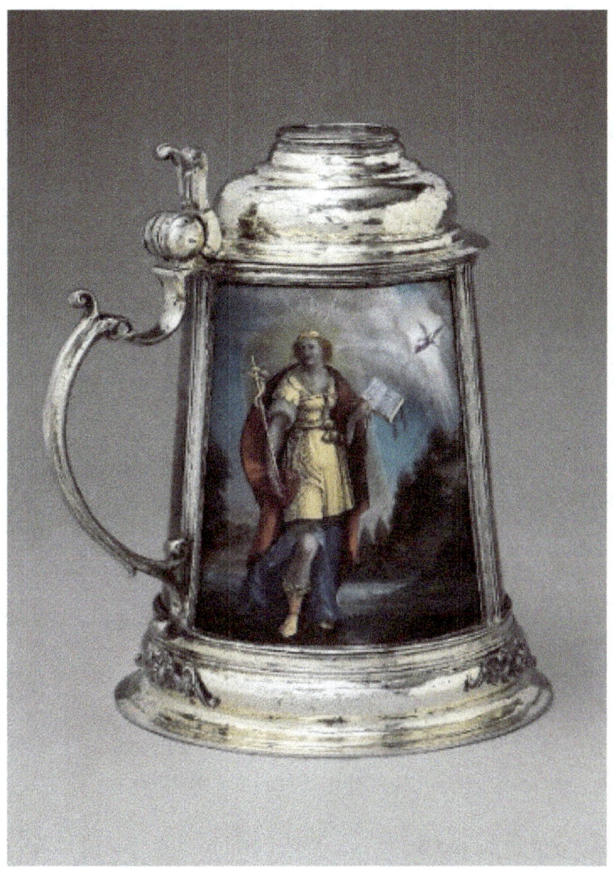

The 1649 CE Swiss *Tankard* shown here creates the illusion of a figure standing inside a tankard. The museum description states, "Better known as painter and engraver, Mayer is thought to have learned the *verre eglomise* technique from the Zurich master Hans Jakob Sprungli." The *verre églomisé* technique involves gilded silver and reverse-painted glass. It is worth a visit to the museum website to see how this works.

Optical illusions, also called visual illusions, occur throughout art, whether intentional or unintentional. As discussed by Janson, illusionist devices are commonly used by artists to highlight specific items.

A more familiar example of an optical, or visual, illusion is this *Night and Day* print based on a drawing by Maurits Cornelis Escher (1898-1972).

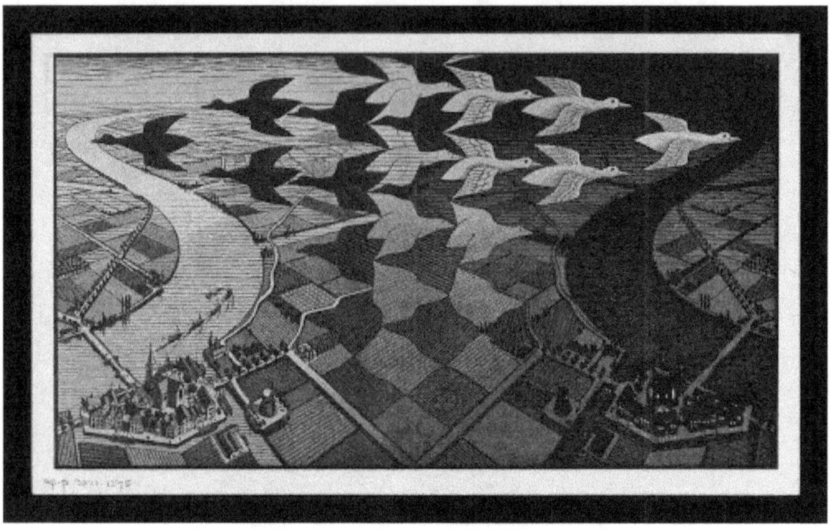

Internet/Wikipedia search terms: optical/visual illusion

Book references: Gross 2002, Luckiesh 1965, Janson 1986

The *Tankard* image is based on printed designs by Dietrich Mayer (1572–1658). The medium is gilded silver, reverse-painted glass (verre églomisé). It can be found at the Metropolitan Museum of Art, Gift of Irwin Untermyer, 1968, Accession Number 68.141.178. The image shown here is in the public domain under the Met's Open Access initiative.

The 1959 photomechanical print *Night and Day* by an anonymous artist is based on a drawing by Maurits Cornelis Escher (1898-1972), who is mentioned on the print. The print can be found at the Rijksmuseum, acquired 2021, Object Number: RP-P-2021-1275. The image shown here is in the public domain under the Rijksmuseum's Creative Commons program.

Candles

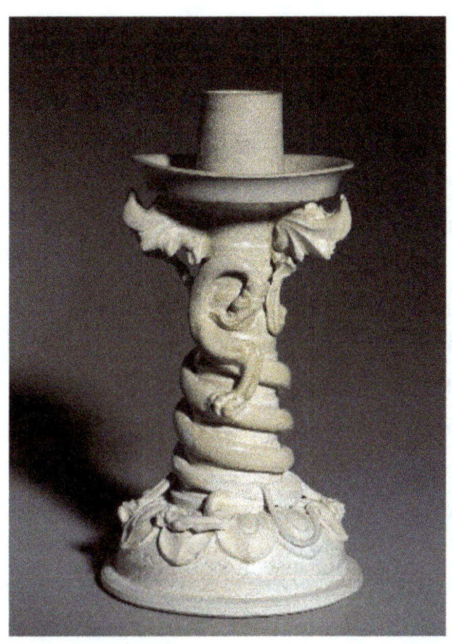

Candles have been around for about 2,000 years, a much more recent invention than the oil lamps from which they must have evolved. This *candle stand* from China dates to around 600 CE.

It is easy to speculate as to how the candle might have evolved from the oil lamp. Both have wicks. The oil lamp has a liquid fuel, oil, whereas the candle has a solid fuel, wax. The candle creates its own oil as the wax near the wick melts.

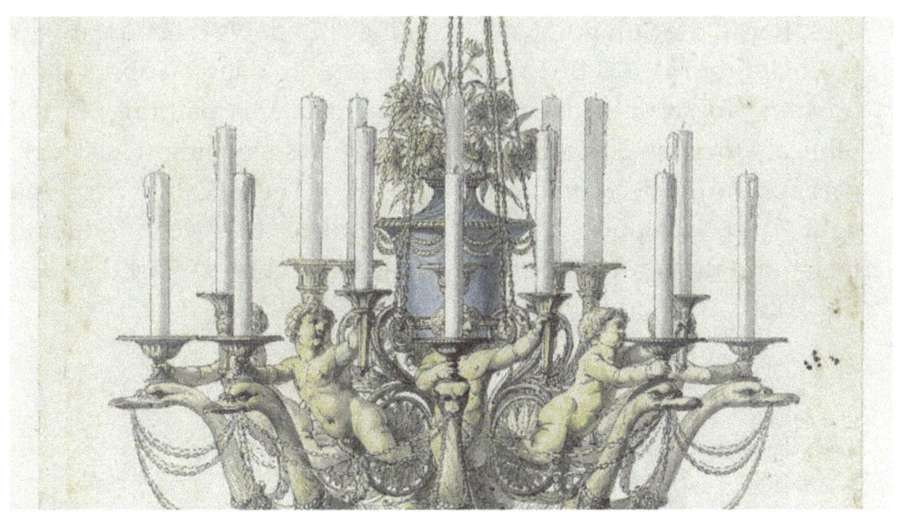

As civilization advanced, candles became the indoor light source for the wealthy. They may have been more expensive, but they were overall safer, and did not require ongoing wick adjustment. The chandeliers found in large halls could be quite elegant, as in the 1784 design on previous page by Jean Démosthène Dugourc (1749-1825). It is hard to imagine achieving a similar effect with oil lamps, although a modern oil lamp can be made to look like a candle.

The 1616 CE painting *Samson and Delilah* by Dutch painter Gerrit van Honthorst (1590-1656), on the next page, tells us a lot about the candle itself. The manufactured candle is not necessarily a work of art, less so than the primitive oil lamp shown earlier. Often the devices that hold the candle, like those shown above, are more significant as art objects. The candle is not a great light source either, in comparison to the modern electric light bulb. It can be, however, if you can afford a lot of candles and a large chandelier like the one shown above.

What is special about the *Samson and Delilah* painting is how skillfully the artist has portrayed the properties of light itself. Moving away from the approximate point source of the flame, the light falls off. Shadows are cast by the three-dimensionality of the figures. Recall the Sun point source in the "Shadows" section of Part II. Euclid (born ~325 BCE) could have taught a lesson about light traveling in straight lines with the help of this painting. In the Biblical story, and in this image, Samson is sleeping. He sleeps, perhaps partly, because the light is so dim! There is almost no blue light, and his body is able to produce the sleep-inducing melatonin that I told about in the "Sleep" section of Part II.

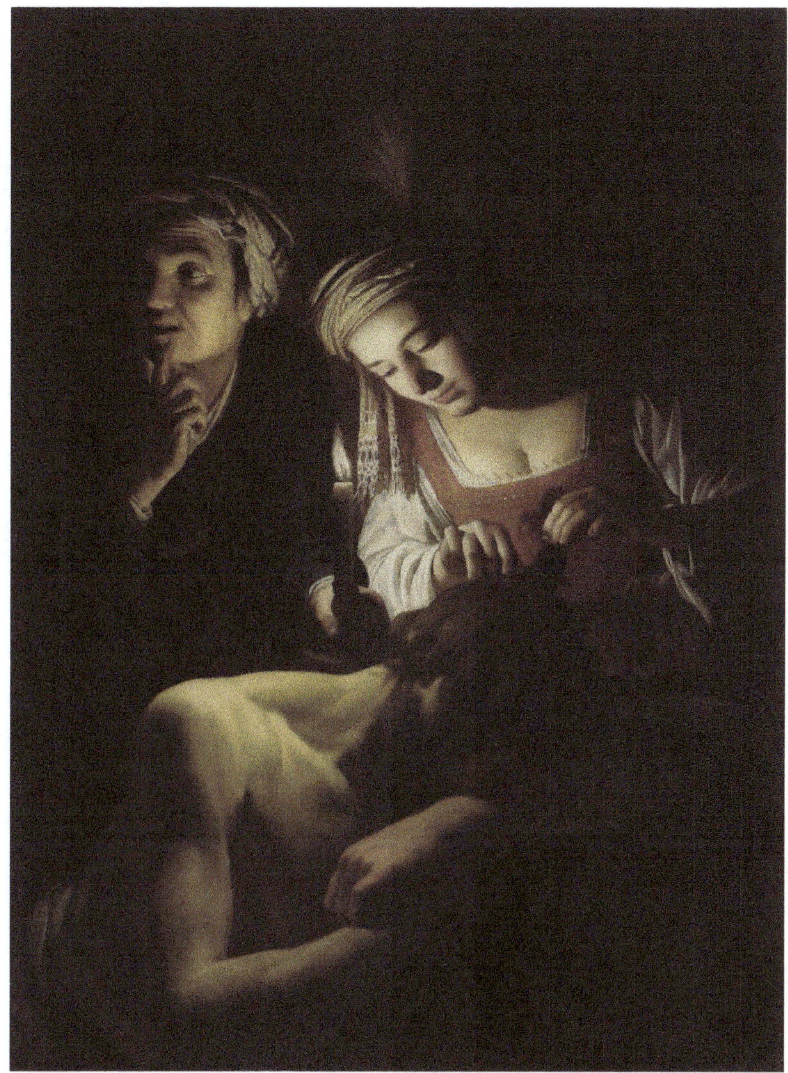

In our modern times, even with convenient indoor electric lighting, candles remain popular light sources for special occasions such as birthday cakes and romantic dinners.

The very modern tradition of lights on a Christmas tree began with German Lutherans decorating the tree with candles, sometime soon after Martin Luther (1453-1546 CE).

Internet/Wikipedia search term: candle

Book references: DiLaura 2006, Kelly 2010, O'Dea 1958

The ~600 CE object *Candle Stand*, China, Sui dynasty (581-618) to early Tang dynasty (618-907), in white stoneware with modeled and applied decoration, can be found at the Cleveland Museum of Art, Charles W. Harkness Endowment Fund, Accession Number 1930.322. The image shown here is in the public domain under the CMA's Open Access initiative.

The 1784 drawing *Design for a Chandelier* by artist Jean Démosthène Dugourc can be found at the Rijksmuseum, purchase 1991, Object Number: RP-T-1991-12. The image shown here is in the public domain under the Rijksmuseum's Creative Commons program.

The 1616 CE painting *Samson and Delilah* by Gerrit van Honthorst (1590–1656) can be found at the Cleveland Museum of Art, Mr. and Mrs. William H. Marlatt Fund, Accession Number 1968.23. The image shown here is in the public domain under the CMA's Open Access initiative.

Mirrors

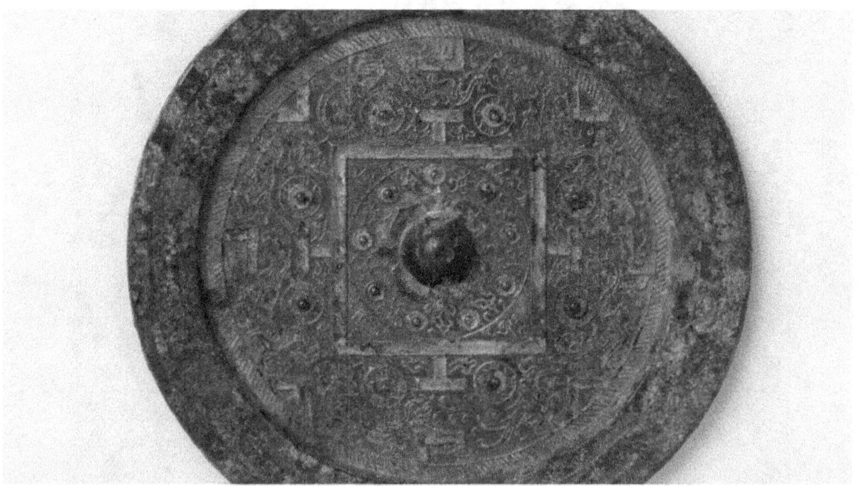

Reflection is a common phenomenon in nature, as discussed earlier, but people also wanted to see themselves in mirrors at home. By the Bronze Age, and the time of Rome, this became possible with bronze mirrors like the ~100 BCE to 100 CE one from China shown above. Its back side, shown, is highly decorated. The intricate engraving on the backside was a common art form of the era, as evidenced by the many examples of similar mirrors found in museums. Bronze is quite durable. This mirror's opposite side, not shown, would be flat, highly polished bronze. It would not have produced great reflections by modern standards.

The pre-1910 CE painting on the next page, titled *Lady Reflected in Mirror* by American artist Carl Newman (1858-1932), shows a fairly modern glass mirror, about 2,000 years after its bronze predecessor.

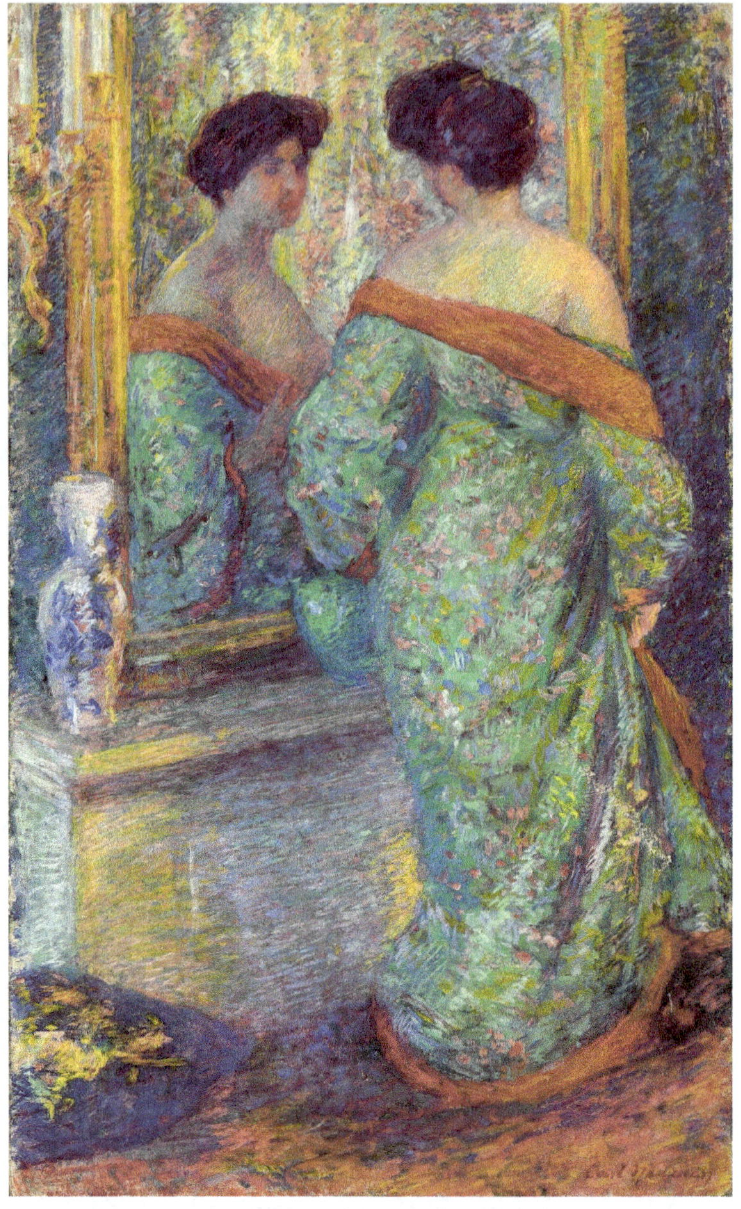

More primitive glass mirrors are thought to have resulted from advances in glass making during the Middle Ages.

Curved mirrors which could concentrate the Sun's rays to start fires were in use since Roman times. These are referred to as burning mirrors. In a popular legend, Archimedes (287 – 212 BCE) is said to have set fire to the Roman fleet during the Siege of Syracuse in 212 BCE using a large-scale burning mirror composed of several smaller mirrors.

The many special refinements and applications of modern mirrors, are topics in any optics course.

Internet/Wikipedia search terms: Archimedes, mirror

Book references: Dampier 1948, Hecht 2017, Janson 1986

The ~100 BCE to 100 CE bronze mirror from China identified as *Mirror with geometric patterns and stylized animals*, can be found at the Rijksmuseum, On loan from the Royal Asian Art Society in The Netherlands (purchase Herman Visser, 1948), Object Number: loan 1972. The image shown here is in the public domain under the Rijksmuseum's Creative Commons program.

The pre-1910 CE painting *Lady Reflected in Mirror* by Carl Newman (1858-1932) can be found at the Smithsonian American Art Museum, Gift of Anna McCleery Newton, Accession Number 1968.121.3. The Smithsonian American Art Museum identifies this image as free to use.

Lenses

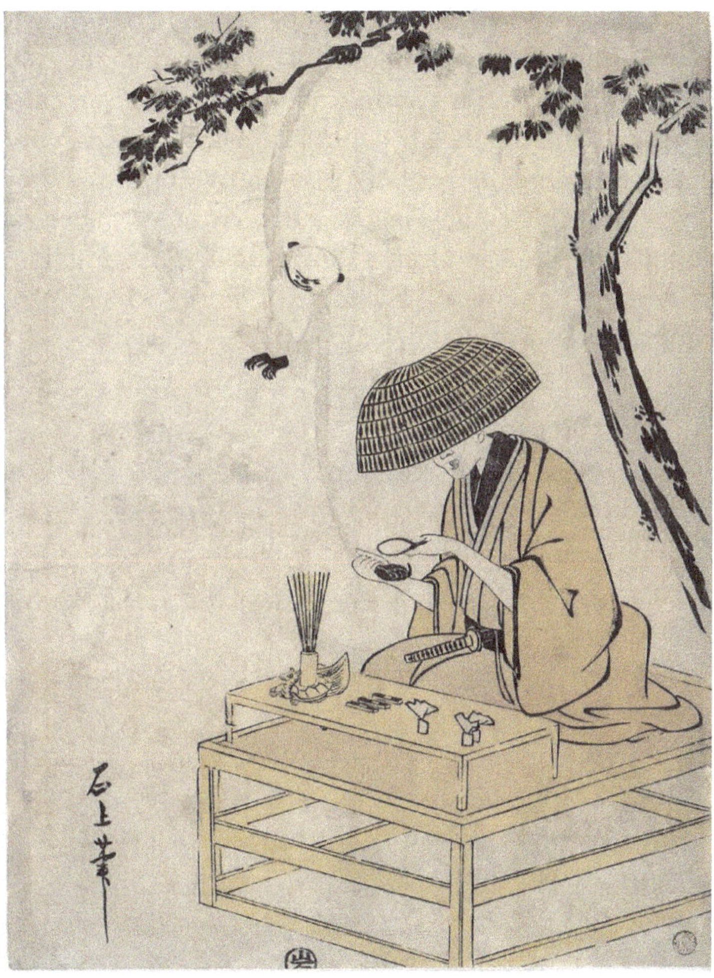

In the 1775 CE woodblock print above, titled *The Magnifying Glass* by Toriyama Sekien (1712-1788), I show a common use of a lens. There is evidence that lenses have been around since the Roman era, at least in the form of burning glasses to concentrate sunlight so as to start fires. Just about anyone today has used a magnifying glass to examine small objects.

As mentioned in the "Refraction" section of Part I, and the "Mirage and Refraction" and "Sunset" sections of Part II, the refraction phenomenon, where light does not travel in straight lines, was not understood by Euclid (born ~325 BCE). The refraction examples in nature are less common and obvious than the examples of reflection. Refraction is complicated, not just because the light does not travel in straight lines, but also because different colors of light are refracted, or bent, by different amounts as they pass through lenses. This color effect is called chromatic aberration. It took about two thousand years after Euclid for refraction to be fully understood quantitatively, and for lenses which correct for chromatic aberration to be developed.

Internet/Wikipedia search terms: refraction, lens

Book references: Dampier 1948, Hecht 2017, Zajonc 1993

The circa 1775 CE woodblock print *The Magnifying Glass* by Toriyama Sekien (1712–1788) can be found at the Metropolitan Museum of Art, Rogers Fund, 1922, Accession Number JP1399. The image shown here is in the public domain under the Met's Open Access initiative.

Camera Obscura

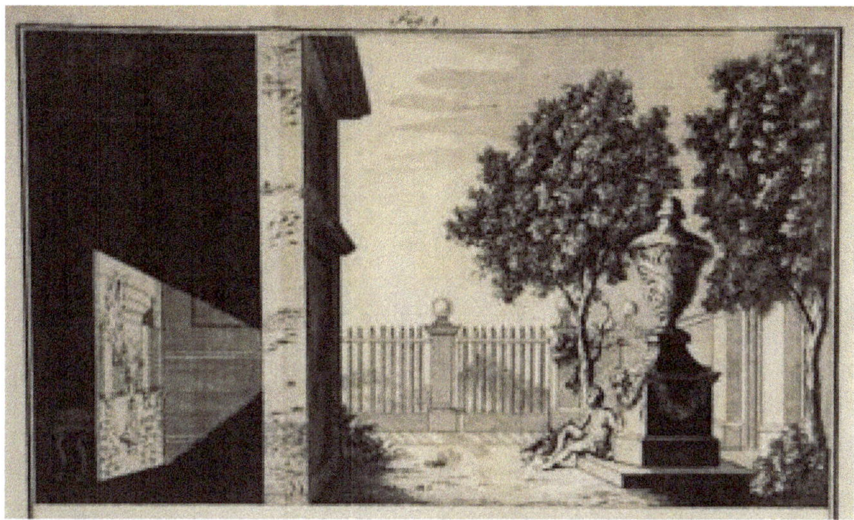

The camera obscura concept dates back to the time of Aristotle (384-322 BCE) and Greece. In this same era, Wikipedia documents that the Chinese were also aware of the concept. Camera obscura translates from the Latin for room (camera) and dark (obscura). The 1755 book illustration above shows how it works. A small hole in the wall of a very dark room enables an upside-down image to form on the wall opposite the hole, an image of what is outside. Again, light is seen traveling in straight lines. With a very small hole, or a lens to provide focusing, the image can be very sharp.

This simple concept has had a large role over the past 2,000 plus years. Landscape artists have used smaller-scale versions of the camera obscura to project the landscape scene onto the canvas so as to get the image scale correct. Leonardo da Vinci (1452-1519 CE) recognized that the human eye is based upon the same concept.

The modern photographic camera, to be discussed in the "Photography" section of Part III, is based upon this concept, hence its name. Simple "pinhole cameras" based upon this principle can be used to safely look at a solar eclipse. Some museum collections show modern-day camera obscura photographs of exterior landscapes projected onto the insides of rooms. There are large-scale camera obscura installations open to tourists in some locations. The tourist can stand inside the camera obscura room and see what is outside projected onto the inside wall. Imagine standing inside the room on the previous page and looking at the wall.

Internet/Wikipedia search term: camera obscura

Book reference: Hecht 2017

The camera obscura principle as illustrated in James Ayscough's *A short account of the eye and nature of vision* (1755 fourth edition) is found in Wikipedia. Wikipedia states "This work is in the public domain in its country of origin and other countries and areas where the copyright term is the author's life plus 70 years or fewer."

Eyeglasses

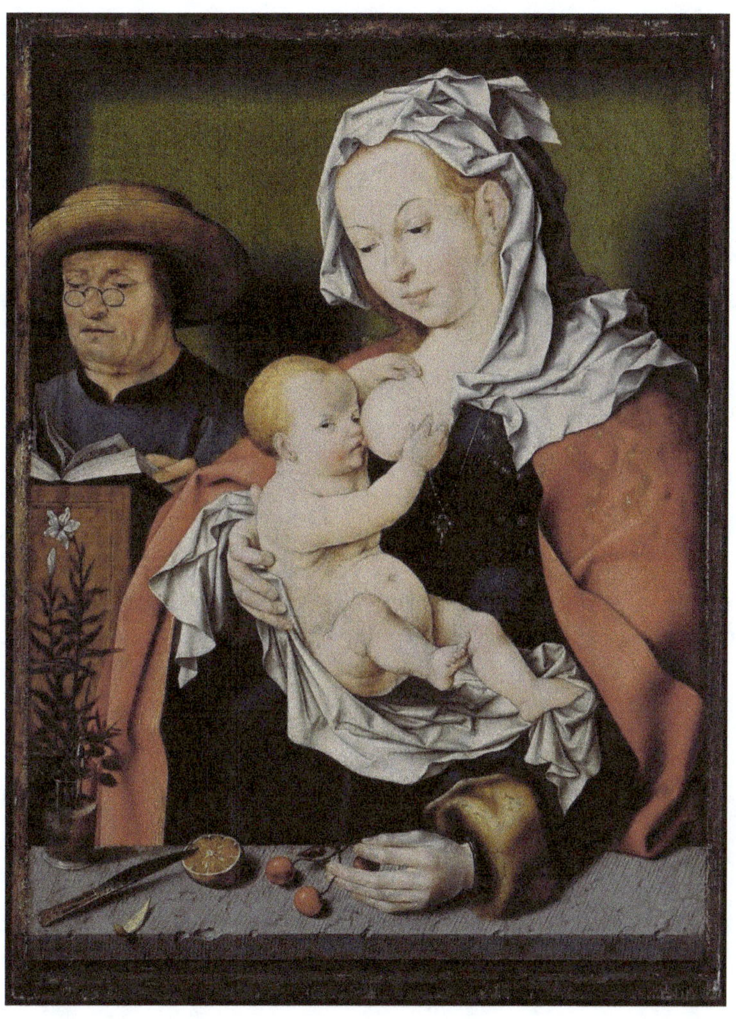

The 1525 CE painting titled *The Holy Family* from the Netherlands workshop of Joos van Cleve (ca. 1485-1540/41) is astonishing. It shows a man, presumably Joseph, the husband of Mary, wearing eyeglasses! To the best of our knowledge eyeglasses did not come into use until around 1300 CE, although primitive lenses were in use for other purposes before that. This was something new, a lens that could be worn! It seems very unlikely that Joseph would have worn eyeglasses 1300 years earlier, and if he had, that the artist would have known this. It is nowhere in the Biblical account.

Eyeglasses, also referred to as glasses, or spectacles, have become increasingly important in our modern culture. Good vision is needed for our everyday tasks, but many of us have imperfect vision, also referred to as imperfect visual acuity. Some of us are nearsighted, others farsighted, for a start. An astonishing variety of eyeglasses is now available to correct for these and many other visual defects, as well as to protect. Now corrective lenses can even be implanted into the eye!

Internet/Wikipedia search terms: glasses, eyeglasses, spectacles

Book references: Ayscough 1752, Hecht 2017

The circa 1525 CE painting titled *The Holy Family* from the Workshop of Joos van Cleve (ca. 1485–1540/41) can be found at the Metropolitan Museum of Art, Bequest of George Blumenthal, 1941, Accession Number 41.190.19. The image shown here is in the public domain under the Met's Open Access initiative.

Telescope

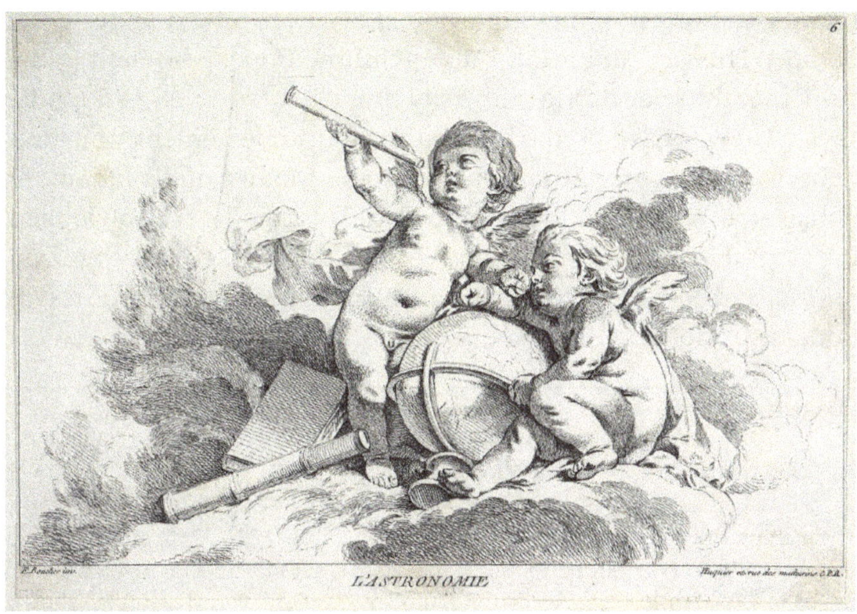

The 1700s French etching titled *L'Astronomie* by Louis Félix de La Rue (1731-1765) clearly shows a telescope, invented in the early 1600s, if not earlier. The earliest ones were simple linear devices like the one shown, involving lenses. Telescopes have evolved considerably in the past 400 years. Astronomical telescopes, including those in space, usually involve very large and carefully shaped mirrors, which avoid the lens problem of chromatic aberration. There are now some very large astronomical telescopes in space.

What astronomers now know about our solar system, our Milky Way galaxy, and other distant galaxies, almost all comes from telescopes. Modern ones operate not just with visible light. Others work with infrared light, radio waves, ultraviolet light, and X-rays.

Galileo Galilei (1564-1642 CE) is known to have had a telescope, which would have been not too long after its first invention. Galileo was able to clearly see the moons of Jupiter orbiting Jupiter, not orbiting the Sun or our Earth. He talked about what he saw. This got him into trouble with the Pope, who held to the view that the everything in the sky orbits the Earth. As Wikipedia says, "He was tried by the Inquisition, found 'vehemently suspect of heresy', and forced to recant. He spent the rest of his life under house arrest." In 1992 Pope John Paul II formally acknowledged the error in condemning Galileo. To this day Galileo is recognized for his central role in the early scientific revolution and observational astronomy.

Internet/Wikipedia search terms: astronomy, Galileo, telescope

Book references: Dampier 1948, Hecht 2017, Tyson 2017

The etching titled *Astronomy* by Louis Félix de La Rue (1731–1765) after François Boucher (1703–1770) can be found at the Metropolitan Museum of Art, Harris Brisbane Dick Fund, 1953, Accession Number 53.600.1079(6). The image shown here is in the public domain under the Met's Open Access initiative.

Microscope

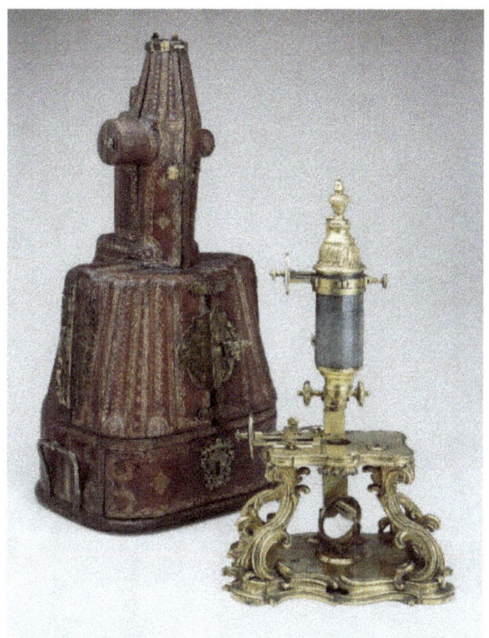

The optical microscope was invented in the early 1600s, in the same era as the telescope, both aided by growing understanding of refraction optics. This one, about 1751, attributed to Jacques Caffieri (1678–1755), with its gilded bronze mount assembly, is clearly a work of art. Its museum description says, "This microscope was made for an aristocratic amateur scientist, who would have used it in his cabinet de curiosité to explore the mysteries of the natural world."

During this time of Enlightenment, the telescope helped us gain understanding of large far-away objects, and the microscope helped us gain understanding of small, close-by ones.

As the sciences of biology and medicine progressed, the microscope played a vital role in the growing knowledge of nature and our bodies at the microscopic level.

Microscopes continue to play a vital role today, not just optical microscopes based on light, but also electron microscopes, which have higher resolution. They contribute to countless advances in science, technology, and medicine.

Internet/Wikipedia search term: microscope

Book references: Dampier 1948, Hecht 2017

The circa 1751 CE *Compound Microscope and Case* has micrometric stage invented by Michel-Ferdinand d'Albert d'Ailly, 6th duke of Chaulnes (1714 - 1769) and gilt-bronze mounts attributed to Jacques Caffieri (1678 - 1755). It can be found at the J. Paul Getty Museum, Object Number: 86.DH.694. The image shown here is in the public domain under the Getty Museum's Creative Commons initiative.

Photography

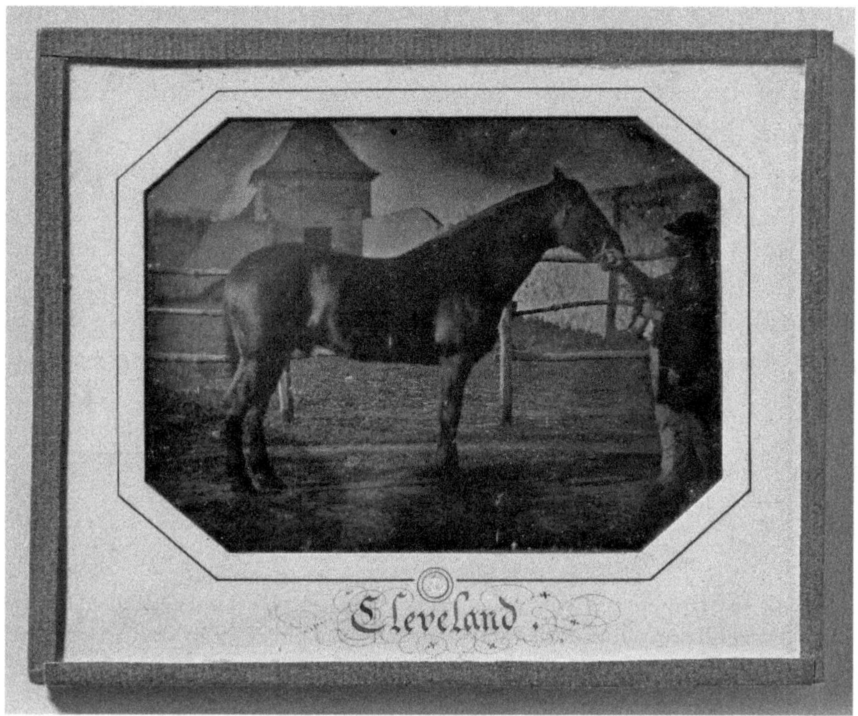

This 1842-1843 CE photograph titled *Cleveland*, which is the name of the horse, is a very early daguerreotype by Louis-Auguste Bisson (1814–1876) using a process developed by Louis Daguerre (1787-1851). The process of the time was not very fast by our modern standards. It is estimated that Cleveland had to stand still for 1 or 2 minutes for this exposure. (It was, however, faster than a painting!)

The development of photography started somewhat earlier, when Thomas Wedgewood (1771-1805) placed some photo sensitive paper in a camera obscura to create an image circa 1800. Hence the camera got its name. The problem with Wedgewood's process is that his images did not have long-term stability. Thus, they have been lost over time. Daguerre's images were stable, and his process gradually improved.

Over the following hundred plus years cameras with film improved, allowing faster exposures, higher resolutions, color, and popular access through companies like Kodak and Polaroid. Cinema, and even home movies, became possible. Today, just two centuries later, most photography is digital, and most people readily take stills and videos on their cell phones. There are many commercial and industrial applications of photography.

Because photography is so effective at capturing realism, graphic artists have been freed to become more adventuresome in modern art.

Internet/Wikipedia search terms: camera, photography

Book references: Janson 1986, Johnson 2019

The 1842-43 CE daguerreotype *Cleveland* by photographer Louis-Auguste Bisson (1814–1876) can be found at the Cleveland Museum of Art, Norman O. Stone and Ella A. Stone Memorial Fund, Accession Number 1991.38. The image shown here is in the public domain under the CMA's Open Access initiative.

Gas Lamps

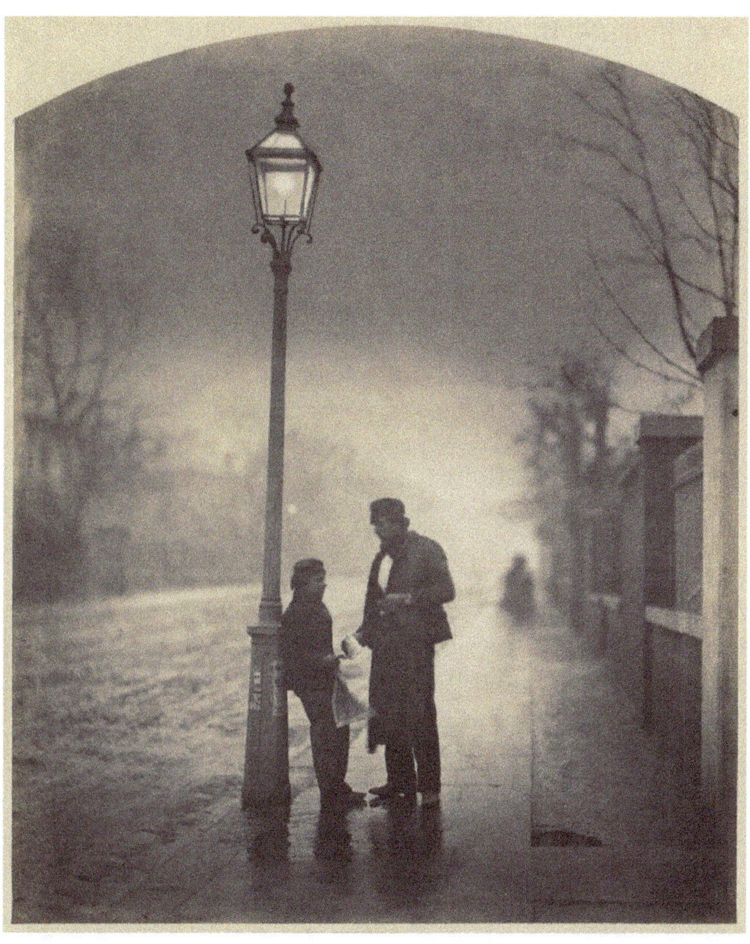

Gas street lighting became common in major metropolitan areas in the 1800s. This photograph, titled *Twilight*, was taken in London in 1859-1860 CE by Camille Silvy (1834-1910). The gas was mostly manufactured from coal at local gas plants, although some natural gas also played a role where it was available. Gas lighting was a significant improvement over oil lamps and candles as an artificial light source because it could burn continuously. There was no oil to replenish, no wick to adjust, no candle to burn out and replace. The gas light did, however, need to be manually lit to turn it on, then manually extinguished.

Gas lighting also entered people's homes in the same metropolitan areas -- anywhere within reach of the gas pipes. This was for anyone who could afford to add the requisite piping to their house, then pay the gas bill. Most people did not live within reach of the gas, or could not afford it. They made do with windows during the day, more modern versions of the oil lamp at night, and candles on special occasions.

Gas lighting was also common in theatres and other public spaces in metropolitan areas where gas was available.

Internet/Wikipedia search term: gas light

Book references: DiLaura 2006, O'Dea 1958

The ~1860 albumen silver photographic print titled *Twilight* attributed to Camille Silvy (1834 - 1910) can be found at the J. Paul Getty Museum, Object Number: 2002.11. The image shown here is in the public domain under the Getty Museum's Creative Commons initiative.

Electric Lighting

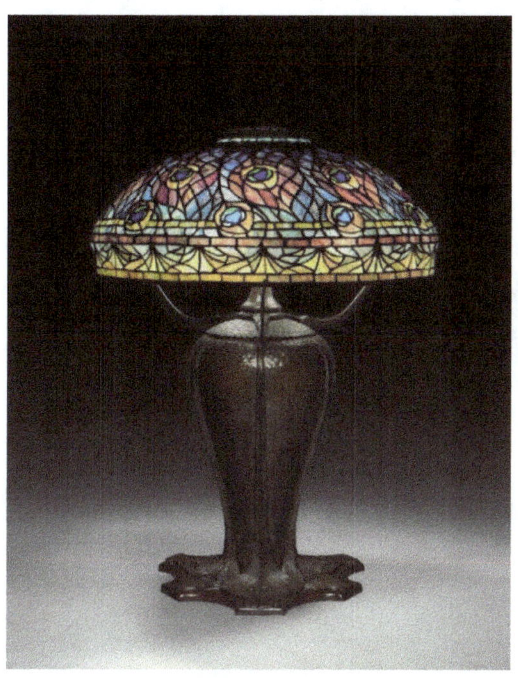

This 1902 Tiffany *Peacock Table Lamp* is a fine example of a practical light source also being a work of art. Its museum inscription reads, "This particular version retains its original kerosene burning fluid apparatus as well as an electric bulb armature. Although incandescent lamp bulbs had become more widely available in the 1890s, most households, even those of the wealthy, were not yet wired for electricity. Tiffany originally designed his lamps with an oil-burning apparatus, consisting of a reservoir and a double wick and chimney, as well as an electric attachment. He cleverly predicted, though, that electric households would eventually become commonplace, so he soon moved to all-electric designs, greatly increasing the illumination and appeal of his lamps."

The early electric light bulbs all worked by making a filament hot enough that it would give off light according to Planck's Law discussed in Part I. The early filaments were carbon, but were replaced by tungsten after a few decades. Tungsten could run hotter and more efficiently.

Electric lighting is an example of an invention whose time had come by 1900. But there is no simple answer to the question of "who invented the light bulb?" The answer depends on who you ask, and how deeply you probe. Humphry Davy (1778-1829) and Thomas Edison (1847-1931) are part of the story. While Edison's 1879 patent is a milestone, even by 1920 only about a third of US households had electricity. Most people did not, and made do with windows during the day, more modern versions of the oil lamp at night, and candles on special occasions. The technology of electric lighting continues to advance today.

Internet/Wikipedia search terms: electric light, light bulb

Book references: Dakin 2021, DiLaura 2006

The 1902 *Peacock Table Lamp* was probably by Clara Wolcott Driscoll (1861–1944) and was made by Tiffany Studios. It can be found at the Cleveland Museum of Art, Bequest of Charles Maurer, Accession Number 2018.281. The image shown here is in the public domain under the CMA's Open Access initiative.

Television

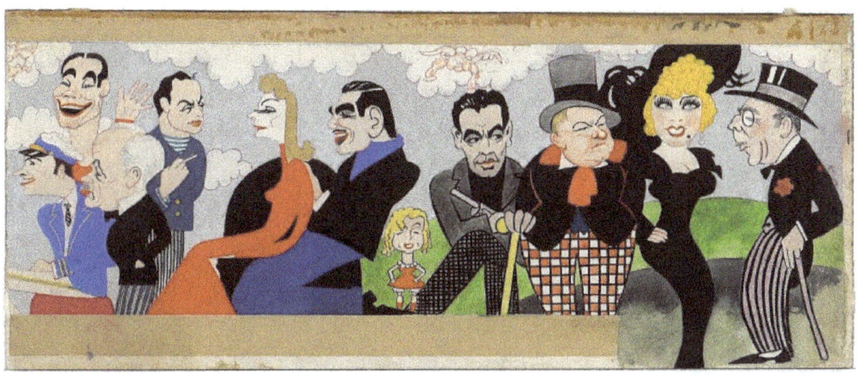

The 1941 drawing *Mural Study #4* by John Decker (1895-1947) shows a number of well-known American stage and cinema celebrities who were eventually able to come right into ordinary people's living rooms through the magic of television. Shown, left to right are: Bob Hope, Joe E. Brown, Charles Winninger, Charles Boyer, Greta Garbo, Clark Gable, Shirley Temple, Humphrey Bogart, William Claude Fields, Mae West, and Roland Keith Young. Once people were able to receive quality visual entertainment at home in the mid-1900s CE, there was no turning back.

Television grew out of photography and cinema to be sure, but also out of widespread light-related science and technology from the century preceding. Most notably, the "picture tube," or cathode ray tube (CRT), evolved from a curious device called the Crookes' tube, which was central to scientific investigations and also to popular public demonstrations involving light, in the mid- to late 1800s. A demonstrator with a Crookes' tube could create amazing color and motion visual effects just by turning knobs.

Other key developments were the ability to transmit first radio, then television, signals through the air. This transmission grew out of an understanding of Maxwell's Equations from that same era. This was an era when science was significantly beginning to drive invention.

Experimental demonstrations of moving image transmission took place worldwide in the 1920s. Widespread television transmission to people's homes began in the early 1950s. Dramatic improvements in picture quality followed with the switches from black and white to color, and from analog to digital technologies in the photonics revolution discussed next.

Television captured people's imaginations and changed their lives. It provided not just entertainment, but also news and education.

Internet/Wikipedia search terms: television, cathode ray tube

Book reference: Dakin 2021

The 1941 CE drawing *Mural Study #4* by John Decker (1895-1947) can be found at the Smithsonian Institution National Portrait Gallery, Accession Number npg_NPG.93.376. The Smithsonian Institution National Portrait Gallery identifies this image as free to use.

Modern Photonics

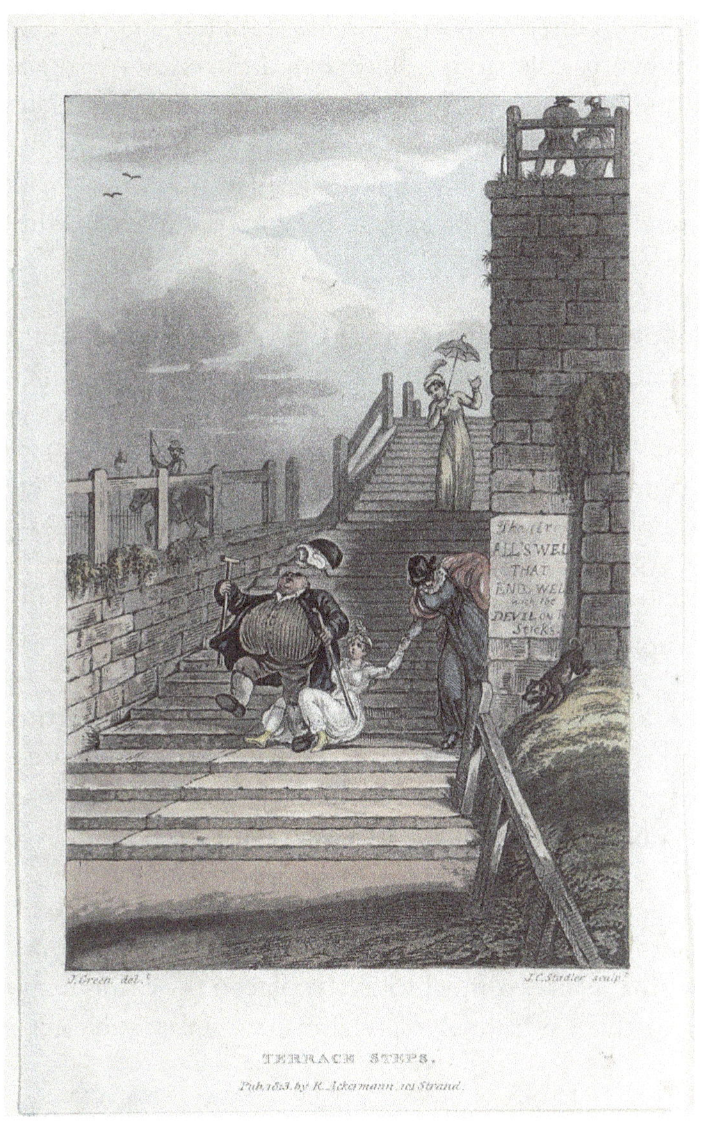

TERRACE STEPS.

Pub. 1813. by R. Ackermann, 101 Strand.

Now, visualize steps with the help of the 1813 CE illustration *Terrace Steps* shown on previous page.

Over the past century, 1920s to the present, scientists have learned that electrons in materials are confined to specific energy levels. The "steps" can be a metaphor for the energy levels. An electron must be given energy to move up to a higher step, and releases energy when it falls from a higher to a lower step. Engineers in the fields spanning solid-state physics and optics have learned to exercise exquisite control over the electrons moving between these steps. This general area is also called photonics when light is involved. Light behaves primarily as particles in almost all these examples.

What follows are gross simplifications of some extremely complicated photonic devices.

A light emitting diode (LED) gives off light when an electron placed onto a higher step falls to a lower step, emitting energy in a photon of light. Little heat is involved, and the devices remain close to room temperature. As a light source, LEDs are quickly replacing the century-old electric light technologies involving relatively more heat.

Sunlight falling onto a similar device can energize electrons, moving them from lower steps to higher steps, effectively generating electricity. This creates a solar cell, a way of making electricity without involving heat, fire, or greenhouse gases.

A flat panel display operates on similar principles to the LED, but with a large matrix of separate LED devices forming pixels. Flat panel displays have almost totally replaced the cathode ray tubes (CRTs) of the traditional television sets described one section earlier.

A solid-state camera operates on similar principles to the solar cell. A matrix of tiny solar cells, creating pixels, forms a digital imaging array where the traditional camera film was previously. The pixels can be very tiny indeed through the magic of modern semiconductor processing. Solid-state cameras have almost totally replaced traditional film cameras. This enables truly instant digital photography.

A laser operates on similar principles to the LED, but with a clever optical mechanism to force all of the light to come out with a very narrow wavelength band, a very narrow color.

Fiber optic cables now carry digital data at higher rates than co-axial electrical cables ever could. Here the light is better understood as waves.

The ubiquitous modern cell phone contains an LED light source, a solid-state camera, and a flat panel display, all in a unit so small that it fits in one's pocket. This was all unthinkable just a few decades ago. Furthermore, the camera and the display in the modern cell phone provide better images than the commonly available traditional cameras and photographic prints that they replace.

This is all possible because the electrons are confined to discrete steps. A continuous ramp would not work.

Internet/Wikipedia search terms: photonics, light-emitting diode, solar cell, flat-panel display, digital imaging, fiber optics

Book references: Hecht 2017, Streetman 2015

The 1813 hand-colored etching and aquatint titled *Terrace Steps* by one of several British artists comes from a series titled *Poetical Sketches of Scarborough*. Artists indicated are Thomas Rowlandson (1757–1827), and Joseph Constantine Stadler (active 1780–1822) after James Green (1771–1834). It can be found at the Metropolitan Museum of Art, The Elisha Whittelsey Collection, The Elisha Whittelsey Fund, 1959, Accession Number 59.533.1620(20). The image shown here is in the public domain under the museum's Creative Commons program.

PART IV

TIME MARCHES ON

"Prediction is very difficult, especially if it's about the future."

attributed to Niels Bohr

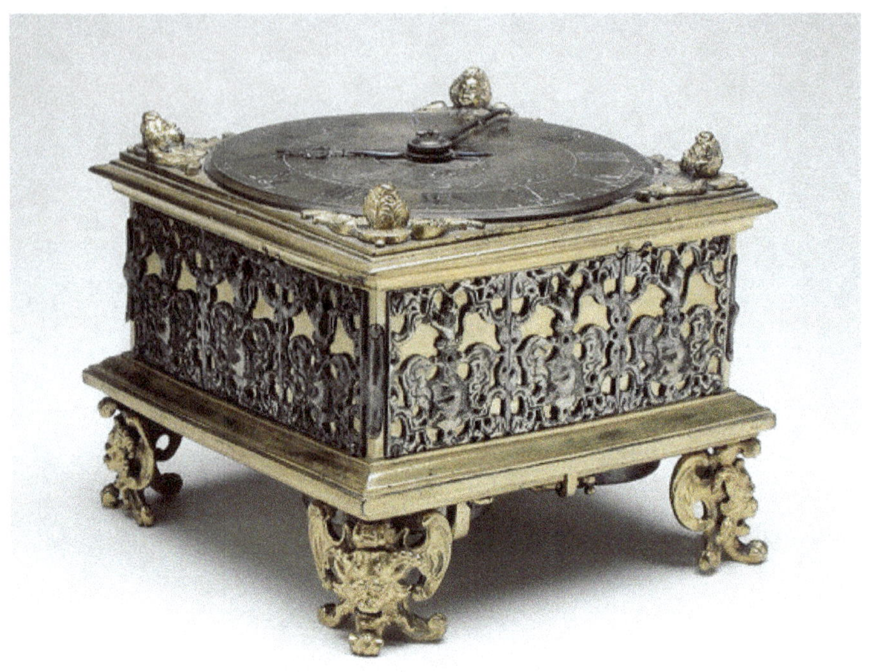

This decorative *table clock* in gilt-brass, silver, and leather was made in Germany circa 1650 CE. It reminds us that our ancestors have been trying to keep precise track of time for quite a while. Once again, a functional invention manifesting as art!

One does not immediately associate time with light. But, throughout most of our Earth's history, the light from the Sun and the Moon have provided the best and most important measure of time – the day, the month, and the year. The timing of the light from these celestial sources has played a key role in many of the evolutionary advances and some of inventions discussed in Parts II and III of this book. Evolution on Earth would have played out differently if the day were much longer, or much shorter.

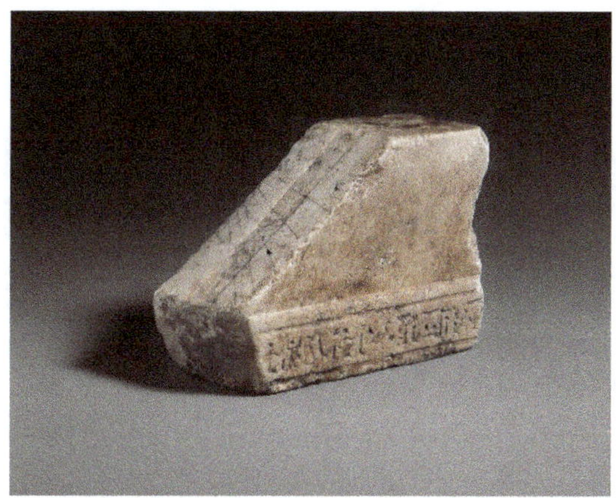

This *Shadow Clock* from the Ptolemaic Period in Egypt 306–30 BCE is an example of a much earlier Sun-based timepiece. Its museum inscription reads, "One of a handful of portable timepieces known from ancient Egypt, this fragment is from the type that told time by measuring the length of the Sun's shadow. Preserved here is the block with a sloping face with a series of parallel and oblique lines engraved on its face to mark off the time. The original piece would also have had a perpendicular block set up in front of the sloping face to serve as a gnomon and cast a shadow."

In so many of the natural phenomena and inventions of preceding sections, an attempt was made to identify the time of the development. The geological, paleontological, archaeological, and historical records only go so far in establishing dates and places. And even with the more recent inventions, for which there are extensive records, there is usually legitimate debate as to exactly when the "invention" occurred and who should get credit. Frequent patent disputes result. There is usually not just one invention, but a series over time, often inspired by one another.

With earlier inventions lacking modern records, it is often not known when they happened, or even where they happened. Cave painting sites are found on many continents. Did the idea arise independently out of the human psyche, or spread from one location? Inventions of the Neolithic Revolution do seem to have taken place in different times and locations worldwide, and independently from one another. Did this, too, emerge from the human psyche? Since the time of the Silk Road, new ideas could travel quickly between Africa, Europe, and Asia, but not to the Americas. The Bering Strait route to the Americas is thought to have closed by then.

Works of art and important artifacts provide a great way to anchor such discussions even if they do not always provide definitive answers. They enable us to see the things under discussion, and notice their features.

Join me in gratitude to the museums for preserving art and artifacts like those shown in the book's illustrations. The museums cited have done a marvelous job of safely preserving these artifacts, documenting their provenances, and making them available to the public. These museum records help to anchor our thoughts and discussions.

With all of this cumulative insight, imperfect as it is, the big question is, "where will time take us next?"

> *"We have literally caught up with ourselves on the human evolutionary pathway; we have reached our present location on the trail... Ahead, we can imagine our species racing forward to some unknown, unfathomable point on the horizon of our future.... The journey will take us where no one has gone before."*
>
> *Feder 2014 – pp 494-5*

Internet/Wikipedia search terms: time, invention

Book references: Bernstein 2008, Feder 2014

The circa 1650 CE decorative *Table Clock* by Johann Sayller (1597-1668) can be found at the Los Angeles County Museum of Art, William Randolph Hearst Collection (49.3.6). The image shown here is in the public domain under LACMA's terms of use policy.

The 306-30 BCE *Shadow Clock* from the Ptolemaic Period in Egypt can be found at the Metropolitan Museum of Art, Rogers Fund, 1912, Accession Number 12.181.307. The image shown here is in the public domain under the Met's Open Access initiative.

Acknowledgements

I am indebted to a large number of people in writing this book. My wife, Karen, has read drafts, and made editorial improvements. Karen and her sister, Cynthia Obermann, are both art lovers, and have helped grow my own appreciation of art. One of Cynthia's paintings is included. Granddaughter Tess Dakin made some helpful suggestions regarding topics and artwork. Reverend Ryan Wallace introduced me to the Polkinghorn book, which reinforced my reconciliation of science with religion and spirituality. Lynn Siefferman introduced me to the Eastern Bluebird's coloration. Jennie Carlisle made some helpful art suggestions. Kate Bouldin provided helpful feedback on the Religion section. Many colleagues from GE Lighting helped me understand and appreciate the many nuances of electric lighting, light itself, and color. Professor Eric Rogers at Princeton gave me a copy of the Dampier book, which piqued my enduring interest in the history. Lessons learned from Roger Williams and John Daverman in previous writing projects have been very helpful. Editor Joan Leib provided fresh eyes and a most helpful editorial read of a near-final draft. I am especially grateful to the museums which retain and provide access to their collections, without which this book would have been impossible.

Annotated References

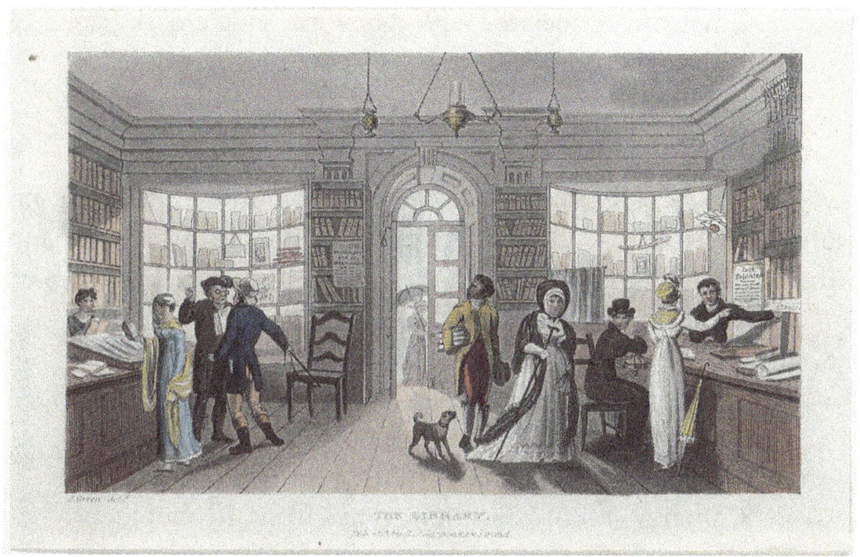

This 1813 hand-colored etching and aquatint titled *The Library* by artist Thomas Rowlandson (1757–1827), after James Green (1771–1834), shows people gathered in a library, long before the days of the internet, Wikipedia, or even electric lighting. Note the full spectrum sunlight coming in through the large windows, and the shadows!

In this era of instant internet access to so much information, it is comforting for an author of my generation to have a great collection of traditional printed books to draw on for fact-checking and to get ideas. Almost all of these are scholarly in one way or another, some exhaustively so. A broad topic like shining art on light relies heavily on quality references.

Armstrong 2005 – Armstrong K. A Short History of Myth. New York, NY: Canongate; 2005.

> This brief book by a well-known scholar traces the history of myth from the Paleolithic period of the hunter-gatherers to the present. Great attention is given to the Neolithic Revolution, which Armstrong associates with the worldwide creation myths. There is less emphasis on specific myths, more on the role of myths in evolving civilization.

Ayscough 1752 – Ayscough J. A Short Account of the Eye, and Nature of Vision – Chiefly Designed to Illustrate the Use and Advantages of Spectacles. London, England: printed by E. Say; 1762. ECCO Print Edition.

> This historic gem, a reprint of which can be purchased online, explains how the eye works. It shows how spectacles can help the near- and the far-sighted. The image found in the Part III "Camera Obscura" section comes from this book.

Bailey 1963 – Bailey DM. Greek and Roman Pottery Lamps. London, England: Trustees of the British Museum; 1963.

> This short book has discussion with images of lots of oil lamps in its narrow range.

Bernstein 2008 – Bernstein WJ. A Splendid Exchange – How Trade Shaped the World. New York, NY: Atlantic Monthly Press; 2008.

> This 470-page book documents the growth of global trade from circa 3000 BCE to the present. While the emphasis is on trade in commodities, such as early trade in grain and silk, the existence of such trade makes it easy to see how an early idea, such as the candle or the mirror, could have spread quickly. The book has a wonderful set of

maps, for instance one showing the global reach of trade in the Roman era.

Bragg 1936 – Bragg W. The Universe of Light. London, England: G Bell & Sons Ltd; 1936.

> This marvelous book was given to me by my father. It summarizes what was known about light science circa 1931 in relatively simple language and with lots of diagrams and images. It was just what I needed as a precocious early teen to become hooked.

Campion 2012 – Campion N. Astrology and Cosmology in the World's Religions. New York, NY: New York University Press; 2012.

> This book deals with how astrology and cosmology have impacted world religions.

Cavalli-Sforza 1995 – Cavalli-Sforza LL, Cavalli-Sforza F. The Great Human Diasporas: A History of Diversity and Evolution. New York: Perseus Books; 1995.

> This book provides a good, scholarly summary of the human migration out of Africa, covering topics such as pigmentation and color blindness.

Clair 2017 – Clair K. The Secret Lives of Color. New York, NY: Penguin Books; 2017.

> This book presents a large number of specific colors used by humans, often in art, from the Stone Age to the present, along with their often-fascinating histories. It has a brief section at the beginning on color vision.

Dakin 2021 – Dakin JT. Wrestling with Light – History, Science and Applications. New York: AIP Publishing; 2021.
> This book covers many of the present topics, but with a much heavier emphasis on the science and on developments since 1900, but almost none of the art.

Dampier 1948 – Dampier WCD. A History of Science and its Relations with Philosophy and Religion. Cambridge, England: Cambridge University Press; 1948.
> This extremely scholarly classic covers science, philosophy, and religion, and their interrelations from Stone Age origins to the early 20th century CE.

DiLaura 2006 – DiLaura DL. A History of Light and Lighting - In Celebration of the Centennial of the Illuminating Engineering Society of North America. New York, NY: Illuminating Engineering Society of North America; 2006.
> This book emphasizes the history of light sources from oil lamps through about 2000 CE, but with no mention of Light Emitting Diodes (LEDs).

Feder 2014 – Feder KL. The Past in Perspective -- an Introduction to Human Prehistory. New York, NY: Oxford University Press; 2014.
> This textbook for a course in archaeology is a wonderful resource for learning about our human history, and how it developed differently around the world.

Gross 2002 – Gross M. Light & Life. New York, NY: Oxford University Press; 2002.

This short book probes several of the topics relating light to life more deeply, with more extensive text, but without art.

Harvey 2005 – Harvey EN. A History of Luminescence From the Earliest Times Until 1900. Mineola, NY: Dover; 2005.
This scholarly 700-page book covers the broad topic of cold light, beginning with the bioluminescent and aurora borealis phenomena discussed by Aristotle.

Hecht 2017 – Hecht E. Optics, 5th edition. New York: Pearson; 2017.
This comprehensive physics textbook is a great source on the broad topic of optics, including many applications.

Hansler 2022 – Hansler RL. Blue Light – Why is it so Special?, Richard Hansler; 2022.
This book summarizes work done by its author researching the role of blue light in our lives, most notably regarding circadian rhythms and sleep.

Harris 2008 – Harris R. Modern Physics, 2nd edition. New York: Pearson; 2008.
This textbook covers the underlying physics of a great many phenomena involving light, starting with the science of particles and waves introduced here.

Janson 1986 – Janson HW. History of Art. 3rd Edition. New York, NY: Harry N Abrams; 1986.

This monumental textbook, lavishly illustrated, would sit well on any coffee table, and provides a great history of art from 8000 BCE to the present.

Johnson 2019 – Johnson WS, Rice M, Williams C, Mulligan T, Wooters D. A History of Photography, From 1839 to the Present. Germany: Taschen; 2019.
This scholarly work contains many photographs, but stops short of digital photography. It is indexed by photographer.

Kelly 2010 – Kelly JF. The Feast of Christmas. Collegeville, MN: Liturgical Press; 2010.
This book reviews the long history of Christmas traditions. It dispels the popular myth that Martin Luther began the tradition of candles on Christmas trees, which likely began with Luther's followers shortly after.

Luckiesh 1965 – Luckiesh M. Visual Illusions – Their Causes, Characteristics, and Applications. New York, NY: Dover; 1965.
This extensively illustrated book categorizes visual illusions (optical illusions), discusses how the eye and brain can play tricks, and gives many different types of examples.

O'Dea 1958 – O'Dea WT. The Social History of Lighting. New York, NY: The Macmillan Company; 1958.
This delightful gem tells about the many light sources over the ages and the ways humans have used them along with some charming anecdotes.

Polkinghorne 1989 – Polkinghorne J. Science and Religion in Quest of Truth. New Haven, CT: Yale University Press; 1989.
> This book, by a former Cambridge (England) physics professor who then became an Anglican priest, provides a reconciliation of science with religion.

Pyne 2019 – Pyne SJ. Fire: A Brief History. 2nd ed. Washington, D.C.: University of Washington Press; 2019.
> This book starts with the beginnings of uncontrolled fire in nature, then goes up through its applications and issues today.

Russell 2017 – Russell PJ, Hertz PE, McMillan B. Biology: The Dynamic Science. 4th ed. Boston, MA: CENGAGE Learning; 2017.
> This monumental 1400-page biology textbook covers several topics of interest here, most notably photosynthesis and vision.

Sproul 1979 – Sproul BC. Primal Myths -- Creation Myths Around the World. New York, NY: HarperCollins; 1979.
> This book contains a collection of specific creation myths from around the world.

Stockton 1872 – Stockton FR. Round-About Rambles in Lands of Fact and Fancy. New York, NY: Scribner & Armstrong; 1872.
> This historic, educational children's book is heavily illustrated by the author and contains the story of the mirage at sea along with the image used here. The entire book is available online through Google Play.

Streetman 2015 – Streetman BG, Banerjee SK. Solid State Electronic Devices, 7th ed. Boston, MA: Pearson; 2015.

This engineering textbook has material on the photonic devices introduced in our last "inventions" section.

Tyson 2017 – Tyson ND. Astrophysics for People in a Hurry. New York, NY: WW Norton; 2017.

This very readable book takes us all the way from the Big Bang through the expanding universe to the present in the world of astronomy and astrophysics.

Waldman 1983 – Waldman G. Introduction to Light – The Physics of Light, Vision, and Color. Mineola, NY; Dover; 1983.

This brief, classic, non-mathematical textbook is written for a short introductory course on light, vision, and colors.

Walker 2017 – Walker M. Why We Sleep. New York, NY: Scribner; 2017.

This book addresses many diverse and fascinating aspects of sleep, including the role of light in healthy circadian rhythms.

Watson 2006 – Watson P. Ideas – a History of Thought and Invention from Fire to Freud. New York, NY: Harper Perennial; 2006.

This monumental 820 page book connects a very large number of ideas over millennia. Context is provided for several of the inventions mentioned here – controlled fire, agriculture, religion, written language, art, cave painting, optics, mirrors, astronomy, and the telescope.

Wetterberg 1993 – Wetterberg L (Editor). Light and Biological Rhythms in Man. New York, NY: Pergamon Press; 1993.
> This scholarly book contains chapters by experts on different aspects of mostly the circadian rhythm mechanism.

Zajonc 1993 – Zajonc AG. Catching the Light: The Entwined History of Light and Mind. New York, NY: Oxford U Press; 1993.
> This non-mathematical book addresses many aspects of light from a somewhat philosophical perspective.

Zuffi 2012 – Zuffi S. Color in Art. New York, NY: Abrams; 2012.
> This lavishly illustrated art book could also go on a coffee table. It introduces many different colors, and how specific artists have used them.

The 1813 hand-colored etching and aquatint *The Library* by Thomas Rowlandson (1757–1827), after James Green (1771–1834), can be found at the Metropolitan Museum of Art, The Elisha Whittelsey Collection, The Elisha Whittelsey Fund, 1959, Accession Number 59.533.1620(16). The image shown here is in the public domain under the Met's Open Access initiative.

Index

About the Author

James Thomas Dakin, known as Jim, was born in 1945, in Pittsburgh, Pennsylvania. He received a B.A. from Harvard College in 1967 and a Ph.D. from Princeton University in 1971. He worked as a post-doctoral student at Stanford University, then briefly as an Assistant Professor at the University of Massachusetts in Amherst, Massachusetts. In 1975 he began a 37-year career with General Electric, primarily in lighting technology. Since retiring in 2012, he has worked as a consultant, and pursued a number of hobbies, including broader aspects of light.

www.ingramcontent.com/pod-product-compliance
Lightning Source LLC
Chambersburg PA
CBHW051454050726
47593CB00005B/2064